To:

_____

From:

_____

Date:

_____

# Living in the
## Light of
# Hope

Milanie Vosloo

CHRISTIAN ART
PUBLISHERS

Originally published in Afrikaans in 2016 by Christelike Uitgewersmaatskappy
under the title *Hoop wat kaalvoet loop*

Published by Christian Art Publishers
PO Box 1599, Vereeniging, 1930, RSA

© 2018
First edition 2018

Translated by Elaine Schiel
Designed by Christian Art Publishers
Images used under license from Shutterstock.com

Printed in China

ISBN 978-1-4321-2883-8

18  19  20  21  22  23  24  25  26  27  –  10  9  8  7  6  5  4  3  2  1

Dedicated to the joyful

*Clara Miya*

who always has a

spring in her step.

# Introduction

True hope is knowing for sure that you are a bit scared and unsure, but still you carry on. You push forward. It is to acknowledge that life sometimes wears you down. Yet you are brave enough to keep on going. Hope is to experience peace amidst the storm, knowing that God's grace is more than enough for you today.

True hope is living in the Light because in His merciful hand, God keeps you safe. He is above, under, next to and in you.

People with hope are people who feel doubtful in the dark and, who still get tired on their life journey but still they choose to believe. They keep hoping. And especially, they keep on loving.

May *Living in the Light of Hope* lead and guide you to experience more of the Father's merciful blessings in your life.

~ *Milanie Vosloo*

# 1 A Small Flame of *Hope*

**H**ope is not a cozy fire to warm up next to, reminiscing about days and nights gone by. Rather, it's a small flame that gives just enough light when it gets very dark.

We can face any challenge as long as we have hope … because then we believe that something positive will come out of it, that there will be healing … that we will experience God's blessing. If we have hope, we can live out our life's purpose with zeal.

Children of the Living God can live their lives fully, knowing that the Father is in control. He will guide us and bring us safely to our final home in heaven. Trust God's wisdom and believe that He is encouraging you every step of the way. The hope He gives is for you!

*Hope is having just enough light*
*for the step you are on, knowing that*
*the Light is leading you onwards.*

Those who hope in the L ORD will renew their strength. They will soar on wings like eagles; they will run and not grow weary, they will walk and not be faint.

~ Isaiah 40:31

God is faithful, by whom you were called into the fellowship of His Son, Jesus Christ our Lord.

~ 1 Corinthians 1:9

Hope will not lead to disappointment. For we know how dearly God loves us, because He has given us the Holy Spirit to fill our hearts with His love.

~ Romans 5:5

*Lord, with my hand firmly in Yours, I put my hope in You.*

*Amen.*

# 2 God Wants to *Bless* You

God is so good to us. His love for us is so great that He sent His Son to die for us. And when the time came for His Son to return home, God gave us yet another piece of Himself – His Holy Spirit.

The Holy Spirit convinces us to accept God's grace and He lives permanently in our hearts. The Almighty Father is with us 24/7, embracing us with His presence … Present to carry us through any circumstance, guiding us in His wisdom, comforting and giving us hope for today and every day.

The wonderful presence of the Holy Spirit who lives in us is just a glimpse of God's glorious grace we'll experience one day.

*As a born-again Christian, you are one of God's beloved children and He will bless you with His unfailing goodness.*

The Spirit is God's guarantee that He will give us the inheritance He promised and that He has purchased us to be His own people. He did this so we would praise and glorify Him.

~ Ephesians 1:14

God the Father knew you and chose you long ago, and His Spirit has made you holy. As a result, you have obeyed Him and have been cleansed by the blood of Jesus Christ. May God give you more and more grace and peace.

~ 1 Peter 1:2

Give thanks to the LORD Almighty, for the LORD is good; His love endures forever.

~ Jeremiah 33:11

"If you love Me, keep My commandments. And I will pray the Father, and He will give you another Helper, that He may abide with you forever – the Spirit of truth, whom the world cannot receive, because it neither sees Him nor knows Him; but you know Him, for He dwells with you and will be in you.

~ John 14:15-17

*Thank You, Father God, for the unfailing love You shower on me today.*

*Amen.*

# 3 You Are *Gifted*

We are all characters in God's story. It doesn't matter the importance of your role here on earth. What matters is the quality of the life you lead as your storyline unfolds.

Ask yourself today: How do I fit into the story of God? Am I the person He wants me to be and is my role in His story good and true?

Who you are and the gifts and talents you have received are not by chance. God knew exactly what to give you with your unique personality. That is why you are who you are and can do what you can do.

For that reason you, in your own special way, take up such an important role in His plan. When you use the talents God gave you, you turn an ordinary tale into an extraordinary story. A story God can smile about.

*Live your life's potential for God's glory.*

"The first servant reported, 'Master, I invested your money and made ten times the original amount!' 'Well done!' the king exclaimed. 'You are a good servant. You have been faithful with the little I entrusted to you, so you will be governor of ten cities as your reward.'"

~ Luke 19:16-17

In His grace, God has given us different gifts for doing certain things well. So if God has given you the ability to prophesy, speak out with as much faith as God has given you.

~ Romans 12:6

Each of you should use whatever gift you have received to serve others, as faithful stewards of God's grace in its various forms.

~ 1 Peter 4:10

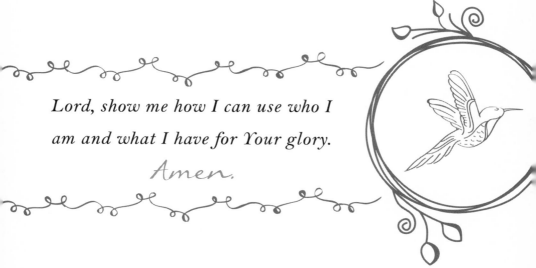

*Lord, show me how I can use who I am and what I have for Your glory.*

*Amen.*

# 4 God *Can Do* the Impossible

Sometimes we are faced with seemingly impossible situations and we know that, humanly speaking, there is not much that we can do. Other times we lose all hope that someone or a specific situation we are facing will get better. In such times we feel like throwing in the towel and feeling sorry for ourselves.

However, these are times when we, as children of the Living God, should be thinking in a whole different way than those who do not know Him. Faith knows that God is bigger than the worst possible crisis we can face; that His power stretches far beyond what we can ever begin to understand and that His love conquerors all: He can make the impossible possible.

Thinking positively can be a wonderful thing, but faith is the realization of something even bigger: It is the certainty that God is always in control and that He has the power to bring about radical change in hopeless situations.

*Never lose hope.*
*Hope is having faith*
*in the darkness ... and in the impossible situations.*

Such people will not be overcome by evil. Those who are righteous will be long remembered. They do not fear bad news; they confidently trust the LORD to care for them.

~ Psalm 112:6-7

For we live by faith, not by sight.

~ 2 Corinthians 5:7

"With God everything is possible."

~ Matthew 19:26

We remember before our God and Father your work produced by faith, your labor prompted by love, and your endurance inspired by hope in our Lord Jesus Christ.

~ 1 Thessalonians 1:3

*Faithful Father, I cling to the hope I have in You.*

Amen.

# 5 Be *the* Best You

The best painting in the world might not have been painted yet; the most moving poem might still need to be rhymed; the best-selling novel of all time might not have been written yet; and maybe some groundbreaking musicals still need to be composed, even better than Mozart and Bach.

Do you get these words? Do you understand that you are the only person who can, in your own way, offer the best to the world? Do you realize that your potential is immeasurable? Do you laugh it off as unrealistic, or do you see the truth of what the Creator has put inside of you?

All of us were created with specific abilities. Some people have abilities that are clearly visible for all to see and admire. Other people's abilities are hidden within the seemingly small things that aren't really that noticeable, but which still make a big difference.

What are you really good at? Do you do it often … or is it something you still need to embrace and realize you are good at?

*Ask the Creator to point out those hidden gems inside of you and to help you turn them into something truly special. Be the best version of yourself that you can be, shining brightly for the whole world to see.*

Sing to the LORD, for He has done excellent things; this is known in all the earth.

~ Isaiah 12:5

To each one of us grace has been given as Christ apportioned it.

~ Ephesians 4:7

Since you are so eager to have the special abilities the Spirit gives, seek those that will strengthen the whole church.

~ 1 Corinthians 14:12

*Open my eyes, Father of Life,*

*so that I can see the abilities*

*You've placed inside of me.*

*Amen.*

# 6 You Are Never Alone

God never leaves us alone. Through the ages, God has been a part of His children's lives in many creative ways. The Old Testament often tells about the conversations He had with His children. Sometimes He whispered softly to them and other times, He spoke clearly and loudly.

In the New Testament, God sent His own Son to earth. On Pentecost, a new phase of God's presence in our lives became a reality. Then God sent His Spirit to ensure that each of His children would be able to experience His presence in a whole new way. The Holy Spirit works through us – the bride – to prepare us for the Second Coming of the Bridegroom.

Your heart can be filled with God's peace, because His Word and His Spirit show us that He has been intimately involved in our lives since Creation. You have God's presence in your life every moment of every day.

*You can be assured ... today, tomorrow, forever:*

*God, in His love, is always with you!*

Behold, God is my salvation; I will trust, and will not be afraid; for the Lord God is my strength and my song, and He has become my salvation.

~ Isaiah 12:2

The high and lofty One who lives in eternity, the Holy One, says this: "I live in the high and holy place with those whose spirits are contrite and humble. I restore the crushed spirit of the humble and revive the courage of those with repentant hearts."

~ Isaiah 57:15

I have set the Lord always before me; because He is at my right hand, I shall not be shaken. Therefore my heart is glad, and my whole being rejoices; my flesh also dwells secure.

~ Psalm 16:8-9

*Spirit of God, I know that You are always with me. Please fill every area of my being.*

# 7 The *Courage* to Give of Yourself

We are not naturally inclined to reach out to people. We would much rather take care of our little world and sit in our corner nurturing the relationships with those close to us. The things going on in the world don't really affect us in our cozy living rooms.

The truth is, we're missing out on God's care – His love, compassion and goodness. Why? Jesus says that God will show mercy to those who are merciful.

Today, people will cross paths with you and you have a choice to reach out to them. This doesn't necessarily have to mean dipping into your wallet; it can simply mean giving a piece of your heart, a word of encouragement, or an act of love that can make a difference in their lives.

Ask the Holy Spirit to give you a heart filled with compassion for those around you, and in whose lives you can make a difference.

*Be the person who reaches out to others in love.*

"God blesses those who are merciful, for they will be shown mercy."

~ Matthew 5:7

No one has ever seen God; but if we love one another, God lives in us and His love is made complete in us.

~ 1 John 4:12

Oh, the joys of those who are kind to the poor! The LORD rescues them when they are in trouble.

~ Psalm 41:1

*Father God, I want to have a caring*
*heart for others. Please help me.*

*Amen.*

# 8 Seek *God* Constantly

God is everywhere … that is if we want to experience His presence. He is in the early morning sunrise that drives away the darkness, the cooing of the pigeons breaking the night silence, the smile of a loved one who is happy to see you, the blessings you receive when reading His Word …

Make every day a day to experience God's presence by focusing your thoughts on Him first thing when you wake up. In that moment, start thanking God for everything you can think of. Praise Him while you're getting ready for the day. Seek His will before you start your daily tasks and embrace His closeness as you continue with your day.

Call to Him when troubles come, pray to Him in your hour of need and sing songs of praise to Him whenever you can. You will be surprised to find out just how wonderfully God answers sincere prayers.

*The more we seek God, the more He will make Himself known to us. This is something Jesus Himself told us. How wonderfully blessed we are!*

"God blesses those whose hearts are pure, for they will see God."

~ Matthew 5:8

Glory in His holy name; let the hearts of those who seek the LORD rejoice. Look to the LORD and His strength; seek His face always. Remember the wonders He has done, His miracles, and the judgments He pronounced. He is the LORD our God; His judgments are in all the earth.

~ 1 Chronicles 16:10-12, 14

I have seen You in Your sanctuary and gazed upon Your power and glory. I will praise You as long as I live, lifting up my hands to You in prayer. You satisfy me more than the richest feast. I will praise You with songs of joy.

~ Psalm 63:2, 4-5

*Omnipresent God, I want to experience more of You in every moment of every day.*

*Amen.*

# 9 Safe *with* God

Children know that they need their parents. Without a shadow of a doubt they know that their parents will take care of them, that there will always be enough food to eat, that they will have warm clothes and that they can follow their lead.

The blind faith of a child. Jesus refers to this as godly faith when He says that God's kingdom was meant for those who have faith like a little child (see Matt. 19:13-15).

Why do you then insist on being so independent if you know that God loves you more than any parent on earth possibly can and that He will always take care of you? Why do you still worry about tomorrow and carry the weight of the world on your shoulders? Surrender every area of your life to God today.

*Trust in the fact that God will take care of you, and go out and enjoy just living!*

"Come to Me, all you who are weary and burdened, and I will give you rest. Take My yoke upon you and learn from Me, for I am gentle and humble in heart, and you will find rest for your souls."

~ Matthew 11:28-29

God will supply every need of yours according to His riches in glory in Christ Jesus.

~ Philippians 4:19

They are abundantly satisfied with the fullness of Your house, and You give them drink from the river of Your pleasures.

~ Psalm 36:8

*Lord, I know that I need You. Please lift this weight off my shoulders.*

*Amen.*

# 10 Getting *Up After* Falling Down

Nobody likes falling down. It hurts, it's uncomfortable and most of all, it's embarrassing – especially if you know people saw the whole thing! Unfortunately, life is not a no-falling zone, and our spiritual lives are in the area where we can most often take a tumble.

Even though we try to live every day with the best intentions and truly desire to follow God's will, we often stumble over our own humanity. We try our very best to live godly lives, but we often realize that we end up doing the things we never wanted to do, or neglect the things we knew we should do.

This human fallibility can only mean one thing: we cannot face a single day without the Spirit of God. That is why we should give our hearts anew to Him every morning. And when Satan tries to steal our goodness by overwhelming us with pangs of guilt, we should reclaim this truth in the name of God.

*Allow God's Spirit to pick you up when you fall down, and to lead you back to where you need to be – in front of the Father's throne.*

The ways of the LORD are right; the righteous walk in them, but the rebellious stumble in them.

~ Hosea 14:9

Let us not become weary in doing good, for at the proper time we will reap a harvest if we do not give up.

~ Galatians 6:9

The LORD directs the steps of the godly. He delights in every detail of their lives. Though they stumble, they will never fall, for the LORD holds them by the hand.

~ Psalm 37:23-24

The faithful love of the LORD never ends! His mercies never cease. Great is His faithfulness; His mercies begin afresh each morning.

~ Lamentations 3:22-23

*Father God,*
*please pick me up*
*when I fall down.*
*Amen.*

# 11 The Art of *Quiet Time*

**D**o you struggle to become still? Is your life so packed full of things and so busy that you hardly have time to sit and relax? Most of us battle with this same problem.

Maybe we need to be reminded that God did not create us to just be busy all the time, but that He also wants us to sometimes just be still, to just live.

He wants us to come into a quiet space before Him, so that we can hear His voice and find peace in knowing that He longs to spend time with us, to share His heart and to embrace us with His unfailing love.

*Make time every day to be still.*
*To sit quietly, to take a breath and to drink*
*in God's love. That is where you will*
*find hope. And peace.*

Jesus said, "Let's go off by ourselves to a quiet place and rest awhile." He said this because there were so many people coming and going that Jesus and His apostles didn't even have time to eat.

~ Mark 6:31

Whether you turn to the right or to the left, your ears will hear a voice behind you, saying, "This is the way; walk in it."

~ Isaiah 30:21

The LORD is my shepherd; I shall not want. He makes me to lie down in green pastures; He leads me beside the still waters.

~ Psalm 23:1-2

Be still in the presence of the LORD, and wait patiently for Him to act. Don't worry about evil people who prosper or fret about their wicked schemes.

~ Psalm 37:7

*Help me in my quiet time, Lord. I want to hear Your voice.* Amen.

# 12 Learn *to Live* Again!

**M**ost of us say that we have to work in order to live, but then we get so caught up in work that we forget to live.

God does not want us to live an out-of-control life. He knows what it can do to us and He doesn't want that for us. When your life starts spinning out of control, take a moment to ask yourself these questions:

- Am I focusing on what is really important, or am I spending time on things that can wait or that I can ask someone else to do for me?
- What changes can I implement that'll make my life less complicated?
- How can I make time for the things with eternal value?

God gives us enough time to do the things that are important. The rest doesn't really matter.

*Ask God to help you live according to His will. Only then can you experience peace.*

I pray that your hearts will be flooded with light so that you can understand the confident hope He has given to those He called – His holy people who are His rich and glorious inheritance.

~ Ephesians 1:18

The fear of the LORD leads to life; then one rests content, untouched by trouble.

~ Proverbs 19:23

"Blessed are the poor in spirit, for theirs is the kingdom of heaven."

~ Matthew 5:3

*Teach me what my true priorities should be.*

*What can I change in my life, Lord?*

*Amen.*

# 13 You Have *Endless* Potential!

It's not that easy for all of us to deal with being "dependent". We often want to be independent, going out and doing things on our own.

Maybe this is why we find it so difficult to live our lives dependent on God. And yet, this is what sets us free! A life of dependence on God is reinforced by the Holy Spirit. In His hand, we experience how He provides us with strength and wisdom that goes far beyond anything we thought humanly possible. He makes us better than we could ever be on our own.

Allow the Holy Spirit to work in and through you to achieve your full potential and to grow more than you ever thought possible. He turns ordinary people into extraordinary instruments capable of so much more. With Him, ordinary people can become great and extraordinary beings.

*God wants to do more than just give you strength. In everything you do and in everything you are, give Him your life. He will make you strong.*

Trust in the Lord with all your heart and lean not on your own understanding; in all your ways submit to Him, and He will make your paths straight.

~ Proverbs 3:5-6

"For I know the plans I have for you," declares the Lord, "plans to prosper you and not to harm you, plans to give you hope and a future."

~ Jeremiah 29:11

I am certain that God, who began the good work within you, will continue His work until it is finally finished on the day when Christ Jesus returns.

~ Philippians 1:6

*Lord, thank You for the love,*
*hope and wisdom You*
*willingly give me to face*
*anything that might come my*
*way. I wholly trust in You.*
*Amen.*

# 14 Fall *into His* Arms

**D**o you sometimes feel like you are standing alone on a swinging rope bridge – you cannot see the other side where safety awaits and you cannot see the flickering flame of hope.

If so, remind yourself: Long before you belted out your first cry as a baby, God was already working on His plan for you. Every day, every moment of your life (even on those days when the rope bridges of life really swung hard and you were overcome with fear), God was already there to hold you. Today, He is still standing right beside you … and tomorrow? You can look forward to tomorrow and the day after that, because God is waiting for you at the gates of heaven.

Your God is faithful. You can trust Him with all your heart. Even now. More than that, you can put your life in His hands and allow Him to catch you when you fall. His arms are never too short to reach out and help, and His grace is more than enough. Best of all, His love for you never runs out!

*Fall into the arms of your Living Father today, lay your heart open before Him and allow Him to give you strength through His Spirit.*

The eternal God is your refuge, and His everlasting arms are under you.

~ Deuteronomy 33:27

We have this hope as an anchor for the soul, firm and secure. It enters the inner sanctuary behind the curtain, where our forerunner, Jesus, has entered on our behalf.

~ Hebrews 6:19-20

The LORD your God is in your midst, a mighty one who will save; He will rejoice over you with gladness; He will quiet you by His love; He will exult over you with loud singing.

~ Zephaniah 3:17

*I feel safe in Your arms, Lord.*

*Keep me close to Your heart.*

Amen.

# 15 Only *One of* You

Have you ever wondered what you're doing here on earth? Why God created you and why you are the way you are?

All of us, including you, were created and placed on earth for a special reason. God created every part of you and knit you together in your mother's womb. He made you unique and special, because He has a plan for your life. That is why He gave you certain abilities, gifts and strengths so that you can achieve your purpose in life.

Never allow negative, worthless thoughts to control your life. There is only one person as unique and special as you – and that is you. Believe it and be the person God created you to be.

*God thinks the world of you. He loves you as if you're the only person in the world.*

You made all the delicate, inner parts of my body and knit me together in my mother's womb. Thank You for making me so wonderfully complex! Your workmanship is marvelous – how well I know it.

~ Psalm 139:13-14

Each of you should use whatever gift you have received to serve others, as faithful stewards of God's grace in its various forms.

~ 1 Peter 4:10

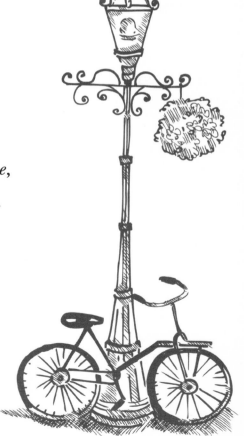

*I praise You, Lord,*
*that I am here for a purpose,*
*that You made me special.*
*Help me to bloom where*
*You have planted me.*
*Amen.*

# 16 What *Really* Matters

We get 24 hours every day to use as we see fit. And once the 24 hours are up, they're gone forever. We can never get the time from yesterday back or stop tomorrow from happening. That is why each day is so important.

What do you think is the most important thing to do today? Do that first. If you picture your responsibilities for the day as a glass jar filled with stones, then you first put in the big stones and fill in with smaller stones. Your first and most important responsibilities come first and then you fill up your day with the rest.

To survive in this busy world, it is so important to spend your early mornings with God. Because time spent with God is never lost. In the quiet moments with Him, you will find the guidance you need to get the rest of your priorities for the day sorted. More than that, you will find strength and energy for the day ahead.

*Make time every day for what truly matters. Especially for spending time with God.*

Whoever obeys His command will come to no harm, and the wise heart will know the proper time and procedure. For there is a proper time and procedure for every matter, though a person may be weighed down by misery.

~ Ecclesiastes 8:5-6

My future is in Your hands. Rescue me from those who hunt me down relentlessly. Let Your favor shine on Your servant. In Your unfailing love, rescue me.

~ Psalm 31:15-16

I pray that your love will overflow more and more, and that you will keep on growing in knowledge and understanding. For I want you to understand what really matters, so that you may live pure and blameless lives until the day of Christ's return.

~ Philippians 1:9-10

*Father, please help me*
*to use my time wisely.*
*Amen.*

# 17 Your Most *Precious* Gift

Time is one of the most precious gifts. Nobody can take it away from you without your permission. You can do whatever you want with it … you can even waste it. When you give of your time to someone, you give them a piece of your life. And that gift of time can make a huge difference in their lives.

May you go about your day inspired by the wise words of William Arthur Ward:

Do more than belong; participate.
Do more than care; help.
Do more than believe; practice.
Do more than be fair; be kind.
Do more than forgive; forget.
Do more than dream; work.
Do more than teach; inspire.
Do more than earn; enrich.
Do more than give; serve.
Do more than live; grow.
Do more than suffer; triumph.

*Give a bit of your precious time to someone else today.*

"Therefore, whatever you want men to do to you, do also to them, for this is the Law and the Prophets."

~ Matthew 7:12

Look carefully then how you walk, not as unwise but as wise, making the best use of the time, because the days are evil.

~ Ephesians 5:15-16

My times are in Your hand.

~ Psalm 31:15

*Almighty Father,*
*my time is in Your hands.*
*Teach me to share my time*
*with others and to use it*
*wisely for Your glory.*

# 18 God Is *with* You

**M**iracles! That is what Jesus' crucifixion, resurrection and ascension are all about. The best of all is that Jesus' coming to earth gave us the assurance that we would never be alone.

Remember, His Spirit is with you each and every day to assure you of your salvation, and to give you His strength and wisdom. That is why you never have to be afraid, uncertain or left to wonder whether you are truly saved. If you accepted Jesus as your Lord and Savior then you are a child of God and His Spirit is in you.

God's Word assures us of this in Romans 8:1-2: "Therefore, there is now no condemnation for those who are in Christ Jesus, because through Christ Jesus the law of the Spirit who gives life has set you free from the law of sin and death."

*When you're in doubt, feel scared or uncertain …*
*know that Jesus died and was resurrected*
*for you, and His Spirit is with you!*

"Teach these new disciples to obey all the commands I have given you. And be sure of this: I am with you always, even to the end of the age."

~ Matthew 28:20

Keep your lives free from the love of money and be content with what you have, because God has said, "Never will I leave you; never will I forsake you."

~ Hebrews 13:5

I have set the LORD always before me; because He is at my right hand, I shall not be shaken.

~ Psalm 16:8

*Thank You, Holy Spirit,*
*for the assurance You give me.*
*Amen.*

# 19 You *Matter* to God

Do you sometimes wonder whether God really has time for you; if He can hear your voice and truly cares about what is going on in your life?

The answers to all these questions of doubt are a thousand times over *yes!* The God who takes care of everything, knit every person together, also knows every thought that goes on in your head. He knows what you're thinking even before you do and feels your pain long before you even realize you're hurt. He understands your questions and doubts even before you utter them. He always listens to your voice, because He has all the time in the world for you!

You are so important to Him that He immediately listens to every cry for help, every song of praise and every doubt in your mind. And He will answer you in His own time and in the right way.

*Talk to God.*

*He has all the time in the world for you!*

"Do not fear, for I have redeemed you; I have summoned you by name; you are Mine."

~ Isaiah 43:1

God who takes care of me will supply all your needs from His glorious riches, which have been given to us in Christ Jesus.

~ Philippians 4:19

"Therefore do not be like them. For your Father knows the things you have need of before you ask Him."

~ Matthew 6:8

*Omnipresent God, what an honor to know You and to be assured that You hear me, You understand and You will answer.*

*Amen.*

# 20 A Life of Abundance

**D**o you sometimes feel dead inside? As if life is starting to lose all meaning and you become discouraged, wondering where you're going?

If so, the Holy Spirit has a message for you: I am here to give you life! True life. A life of abundance, joy and peace … an eternal life. The Spirit of God gives weary souls new hope and to those who feel discouraged a new perspective, new answers … renewed strength.

He comforts those who are sad, strengthens those who feel weak, and gives wisdom to those who feel like there is no help. "I pray that from His glorious, unlimited resources He will empower you with inner strength through His Spirit" (Eph. 3:16).

*The Spirit of God*
*gives weathered trees new life.*
*Allow Him to do the same for you.*

The Spirit is God's guarantee that He will give us the inheritance He promised and that He has purchased us to be His own people. He did this so we would praise and glorify Him.

~ Ephesians 1:14

If the Spirit of Him who raised Jesus from the dead dwells in you, He who raised Christ Jesus from the dead will also give life to your mortal bodies through His Spirit who dwells in you.

~ Romans 8:11

Out of His fullness we have all received grace in place of grace already given.

~ John 1:16

*Spirit of God, help me to live*
*abundantly in Your strength.*
*Amen.*

# 21 God *Loves* You

**G**od loves you so much that He wants to connect with you in different ways every day. He speaks to you through:

- *His Creation.* Listen for His voice in the whisper of gentle rain and the lapping sound of a stream. Experience His might in the picture-perfect scenery of the changing seasons.
- *His Word.* Whatever you may need, the Word has an abundance of answers, advice and comfort to give you. Make time to discover it every day.
- *His Spirit.* In the stillness of your prayers, in the hustle and bustle of each day, and even in the times you try to live your life without Him, the Holy Spirit is with you.

The children of God are highly favored and blessed. We have the gift of the omniscient, omnipresent, omnipotent God who longs to bless us every moment of every single day.

*Take time out to hear, see and experience this awe-inspiring God we serve. Your soul will be refreshed as a result!*

For this very reason, make every effort to add to your faith goodness; and to goodness, knowledge; and to knowledge, self-control; and to self-control, perseverance; and to perseverance, godliness; and to godliness, mutual affection; and to mutual affection, love.

~ 2 Peter 1:5-7

"I have loved you even as the Father has loved Me. Remain in My love."

~ John 15:9

"If that is how God clothes the grass of the field, which is here today and tomorrow is thrown into the fire, will He not much more clothe you – you of little faith?"

~ Matthew 6:30

*Almighty Father, I want to know You more! Teach me to truly feel, hear and see You in the everyday things of life.*
*Amen.*

# 22 God's Creation Rejoices!

It's so easy to see and hear God ... if only we'd open our eyes and ears. Because He is everywhere. Just ask yourself: Are you still greeted by the sun's warm rays when you wake up in the morning? Can you hear the birds singing at the dawn of each new day? Can you feel the wind brush softly through your hair? Do you delight in the beauty of a unique flower, hear the joy when people laugh and feel your heart warmed by love?

Our way of living can so easily leave us blind, deaf and heartless. That is why it is so important for us to take time to enjoy God's creation – even in the hustle and bustle of a material world. This is where we find God. In the silence we will be able to hear nature's symphony singing His praises, see the masterpieces He created, and experience complete inner peace in His presence.

*Make time to hear and see*
*God in the world around you every day.*

Praise the LORD! Let all that I am praise the LORD.
I will praise the LORD as long as I live. I will sing
praises to my God with my dying breath.

~ Psalm 146:1-2

For His invisible attributes, namely, His eternal
power and divine nature, have been clearly per-
ceived, ever since the creation of the world, in
the things that have been made. So they are
without excuse.

~ Romans 1:20

Your righteousness is like the mountains of God;
Your judgments are like the great deep; man and
beast You save, O LORD. How precious is Your
steadfast love, O God! The children of mankind
take refuge in the shadow of Your wings.

~ Psalm 36:6-7

*Creator God, I praise You today*
*for Your amazing love!*
*Amen.*

# 23 You Are Cherished

Have you ever felt like the weakest link? Hopeless? Unworthy? Unqualified? Maybe that's exactly how you're feeling right now. It's hard to make peace with feelings of worthlessness and failure. But you are never worthless in God's eyes! On the contrary, He cherishes you and loves you endlessly.

The tax collector Zacchaeus was a small man carrying a big burden of sin (Luke 19:1-10). He was, after all, the chief tax collector, an out-and-out scoundrel. But he was so curious to see what Jesus looked like that he climbed in a tree to get a better view. And that was all Jesus needed to call him down so that He could change Zacchaeus's life.

*If Jesus saw something special enough in a tax collector like Zacchaeus to call him to service, how much more does He see goodness and worth in you!*

The LORD has appeared of old to me, saying: "Yes, I have loved you with an everlasting love; therefore with loving-kindness I have drawn you."

~ Jeremiah 31:3

What are mere mortals that You should think about them, human beings that You should care for them? Yet You made them only a little lower than God and crowned them with glory and honor.

~ Psalm 8:4-5

God is so rich in mercy, and He loved us so much, that even though we were dead because of our sins, He gave us life when He raised Christ from the dead. (It is only by God's grace that you have been saved!)

~ Ephesians 2:4-5

*Lord Jesus, use me today for Your glory.*
*Amen.*

# 24 *Spiritually* Strong

To get fit is hard work. And staying fit can be even more difficult. You have to make time for it in your busy schedule. Being prayer-fit is also not so easy.

Yet I want to encourage you to keep trying, persevere and keep turning to God, spending regular time with Him in prayer. You'll be surprised to discover how much joy can be found in spending time with the God who knows you, loves you, and embraces you in His grace. You'll experience deep inner peace during tumultuous and busy times, unequalled wisdom in every situation and wonderful joy.

This "spending time with God" exercise routine will not only give you strong prayer muscles and a powerful relationship with God; it'll also get you hooked on your quiet times with Him. What a wonderful habit to set!

*You'll discover that continuous contact with the Spirit of God is wonderful and refreshing!*

Be strong in the Lord and in His mighty power.

~ Ephesians 6:10

You, beloved, building yourselves up in your most holy faith and praying in the Holy Spirit, keep yourselves in the love of God, waiting for the mercy of our Lord Jesus Christ that leads to eternal life.

~ Jude 20-21

Those who look to Him for help will be radiant with joy; no shadow of shame will darken their faces. Fear the LORD, you His godly people, for those who fear Him will have all they need.

~ Psalm 34:5, 9

*Lord, shape my soul in such a way that it'll be fit and healthy for the glory of Your name.*

*Amen.*

# 25 The Crown of Life

**D**o you know that you are royalty? If you have accepted Jesus as your Savior, your Father is the King. You have been crowned and this means:

- You are free. Christ made you in a special way and uniquely you.
- You are forgiven. God has completely forgiven you, so forgive others and yourself.
- You can be confident, because God is always with you. He is there to help you and He wants to use you in His plan.
- You can enjoy life, because Christ loves you so much that He died for you on the cross.
- You can experience peace, because He takes care of you. Day after day He carries you.

*Live today like a child of a King,*
*because that is exactly who you are!*

Praise be to the Lord, to God our Savior, who daily bears our burdens. Our God is a God who saves; from the Sovereign LORD comes escape from death.

~ Psalm 68:19-20

Stand fast therefore in the liberty by which Christ has made us free, and do not be entangled again with a yoke of bondage.

~ Galatians 5:1

Blessed is the one who perseveres under trial because, having stood the test, that person will receive the crown of life that the Lord has promised to those who love Him.

~ James 1:12

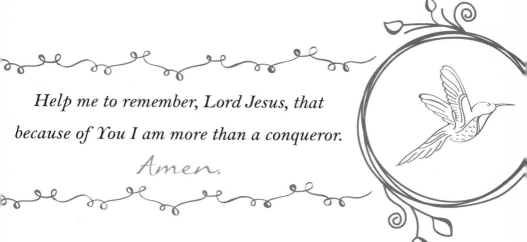

*Help me to remember, Lord Jesus, that because of You I am more than a conqueror.*

Amen.

# 26 Food *for* the Soul

To think you don't even have to use Facebook, Twitter or e-mail to talk to God! You're connected to Him the moment you focus your thoughts on Him. And God, unlike people, is never too far away or too busy to listen to your heart's desires.

What is great about the Spirit of God is that He knows each and every one of us personally; He understands us, loves us, and is so tuned into our needs that it feels like we're His only priority. He knows who you are, your troubles, your worries and your pain. He also knows your dreams, expectations, joys and successes.

You have a heavenly Gift! A Friend who is so great that you can talk to Him 24/7 to ask advice, guidance, encouragement, wisdom and comfort. This Special Gift – the Holy Spirit – God gave to you so that you can experience His deep love for you.

*Enjoy the gift*
*of having God right beside you every day!*

"And now I will send the Holy Spirit, just as My Father promised. But stay here in the city until the Holy Spirit comes and fills you with power from heaven."

~ Luke 24:49

The Holy Spirit helps us in our weakness. For example, we don't know what God wants us to pray for. But the Holy Spirit prays for us with groanings that cannot be expressed in words.

~ Romans 8:26

Since we live by the Spirit, let us keep in step with the Spirit.

~ Galatians 5:25

*Holy Spirit, remain*
*the focus of my*
*thoughts and life today.*
*Amen.*

# 27 Look *Forward* to the **Future**

**D**o you have hope? Do you hope expectantly with your eyes firmly set on the future? Or do you get so busy trying to get through the day that you forget to look a little further? We often get so busy with the things of the world that we become short-sighted and only focus on now. And this while God's grace is made available to us in so many different ways and while He waits to shower us with His blessings.

God promises us more than just blessings here on earth. He promises to one day make us very rich when we share in His heavenly glory and blessings.

May you look further than your everyday to-do list to see the beauty and goodness of that which the Spirit of God places around you. Pray that God will open your eyes to the wonderful grace He blesses you with every day.

*Your heavenly Father has prepared a special blessing for you … live your life, expecting His promises of blessing to come true.*

I pray that your hearts will be flooded with light so that you can understand the confident hope He has given to those He called – His holy people who are His rich and glorious inheritance.

~ Ephesians 1:18

May the God of hope fill you with all joy and peace as you trust in Him, so that you may overflow with hope by the power of the Holy Spirit.

~ Romans 15:13

Oh, fear the LORD, you His saints! There is no want to those who fear Him.

~ Psalm 34:9

*When I look at everything You*
*do for me here one earth, Father,*
*I know that I can look with*
*expectation at all that You have*
*for me in heaven. Thank You for*
*Your abundant blessings.*
*Amen.*

# 28 Hope Seeks *the* Spark

Legend has it that the harp that Hope plays only has one string, yet she continues to play while the storm rages on. Hope is not blind to the missing strings in your life. It plays around those missing strings. Because real hope is not just a legendary tale to comfort us. Rather, it's having the courage to stare reality in the face, accept it and know that things will get better.

One of the best ways to think yourself out of what seems like a hopeless situation is to remind yourself of …

- the previous times you felt like this, but were able to keep playing your harp with missing strings and all. Can you remember how that little bit of hope gave you renewed strength?
- how surprised you were to realize the different ways in which God carried you through?
- what you felt when your problems were resolved. Cling to the knowledge that you will feel that way again.

*Hope looks for that little spark deep within your heart and turns it into a burning flame.*

The apostles said to the Lord, "Show us how to increase our faith."

~ Luke 17:5

Blessed are those whose help is the God of Jacob, whose hope is in the LORD their God.

~ Psalm 146:5

Therefore do not throw away your confidence, which has a great reward. For you have need of endurance, so that when you have done the will of God you may receive what is promised.

~ Hebrews 10:35-36

*Lord Jesus, teach me to hope in You always. Help me to believe!*

*Amen.*

# 29 Grow *with* Joy

**I**f you were a plant, what plant would you be? Would you be a gentle poppy, a joyful daisy or a strong rose? Or perhaps a hardened succulent that can stand strong no matter the weather, shrubbery that gives off a wonderful smell, or maybe a wild flower that surprises everyone with your friendliness? Maybe you're more like a vine that covers the ugly walls in life with your love, or a massive tree giving shelter to others from the heat.

It doesn't really matter what kind of person you are. What matters is that there is nobody quite like you. And no one can do what you can do. No one else can make the difference you can in the place and among the people you've been planted. Do you understand? Can you hear the Holy Spirit telling you that because you are who you are, He wants to use you right where you are.

*God wants to bless your uniqueness and use you in His kingdom. Be happy to grow, using the wonderful and unique characteristics God has placed in front of you.*

When you sow, you do not plant the body that will be, but just a seed, perhaps of wheat or of something else. But God gives it a body as He has determined, and to each kind of seed He gives its own body.

~ 1 Corinthians 15:37-38

I am like an olive tree flourishing in the house of God; I trust in God's unfailing love for ever and ever.

~ Psalm 52:8

Those who are planted in the house of the Lord shall flourish in the courts of our God. They shall still bear fruit in old age; they shall be fresh and flourishing, to declare that the Lord is upright; He is my rock, and there is no unrighteousness in Him.

~ Psalm 92:13-16

*Lord, teach me the art of living an abundant life as the best version of myself that I can be.*

*Amen.*

# 30 A *New* Tomorrow

**W**e all wonder about the future. We struggle with questions about the safety, health, care and future expectations of ourselves and our loved ones.

When you feel uncertain or fearful of the future or your loved one's future, it is time to meditate on the promises of God in His Word. Promises like Psalm 91:14-15, where the Lord Himself says, "I will rescue those who love Me. I will protect those who trust in My name. When they call on Me, I will answer; I will be with them in trouble. I will rescue and honor them."

Children of God are not immune to worries and doubts. But God's children approach life differently. We face life with hope – the unfailing truth – that God will be with us no matter our circumstances.

*A person can withstand any storm as*
*long as they're looking at it through the*
*lens of hope. The kind of*
*hope that knows that God is already there!*

Yet this I call to mind and therefore I have hope: Because of the LORD's great love we are not consumed, for His compassions never fail. They are new every morning; great is Your faithfulness.

~ Lamentations 3:21-23

"For I know the plans I have for you," says the LORD. "They are plans for good and not for disaster, to give you a future and a hope."

~ Jeremiah 29:11

The LORD takes pleasure in those who fear Him, in those who hope in His mercy.

~ Psalm 147:11

*Lord, thank You that I can trust*
*You every day for the rest of my life.*
*Amen.*

# 31 God *Is on* Your Side

**W**hat a wonderful experience it must have been for the Israelites when God parted the Red Sea so they could walk through on dry land. Even more so when the wall of water closed up behind them and swallowed their enemies whole. The fact is, when God fights on our behalf, He makes things happen that go far beyond what we could ever hope to understand.

If we know how great the Almighty Father is, why do we still worry so much? Why do we allow our circumstances to make us panic and fret about how it'll all turn out in the end? Because we, subconsciously, find it almost impossible to surrender all of our problems to God. We still doubt. Because we are human, we find it difficult to trust completely.

Allow the Holy Spirit to fill your heart with His peace. God can wipe away the mountain of problems in front of you.

*Pray that God's Spirit will give you the ability to completely trust that the Almighty Father can do the impossible.*

The LORD will fight for you; you need only to be still.

~ Exodus 14:14

Protect me, for I am devoted to You. Save me, for I serve You and trust You. You are my God.

~ Psalm 86:2

Though I walk in the midst of trouble, You will revive me; You will stretch out Your hand against the wrath of my enemies, and Your right hand will save me.

~ Psalm 138:7

*Heavenly Father, please forgive my unbelief and doubt, and give me the peace that comes with trusting You wholeheartedly.*

*Amen.*

# 32 Focus on God

"Y ou will get through this," we encourage a friend who finds herself amid a mighty storm. "Don't give up," we tell our children when they have a challenging mountain they need to climb. We know by now that difficult times don't last forever.

But even though we encourage people with this truth, we find it hard to embrace it ourselves when we go through trying times. We also struggle to see the light at the end of the tunnel and the silver lining around the dark cloud up ahead.

How are we then supposed to get through a crisis?

- Focus less on the problems and more on God – the Almighty God who keeps heaven and earth in the palm of His hand.
- Seek His presence. Talk to Him, look for answers in His Word and ask other believers to pray for you.
- Listen to the wisdom God gives you and do what He asks of you.

*Make sure that when you go through trials and you have to persevere, that you stay under God's blanket of grace. That is the one place where you'll be safe.*

Do not be afraid. Stand firm and you will see the deliverance the LORD will bring you today.

~ Exodus 14:13

Why, my soul, are you downcast? Why so disturbed within me? Put your hope in God, for I will yet praise Him, my Savior and my God.

~ Psalm 42:11

We can rejoice, too, when we run into problems and trials, for we know that they help us develop endurance. And endurance develops strength of character, and character strengthens our confident hope of salvation.

~ Romans 5:3-4

*Lord of Light, I don't want to live without Your grace for a single second. Please guide and fill me with more of You.*

*Amen.*

# 33 Believe *That* God Can

As long as you have hope, you can move forward no matter the situation you find yourself in. Because hope gives you the strength to put one foot in front of the other.

The fact is, there is always a reason to hope. Because there will always be a tomorrow – a tomorrow where God will be with us too. Tomorrow might not bring everything you hoped for … or perhaps you'll have even more reason to doubt. Yet one thing we know for certain: we worship an unshakable God.

It doesn't matter how far you've fallen, how big your problems are, or how dreary your situation seems, you can keep on hoping. Because you worship a God who can do anything. He can break down walls and rebuild them in a moment.

He can save those who are lost and embrace them in His loving arms, and He can lead anyone who is willing on the road to salvation.

*Faith is hope in action. It is knowing beyond a shadow of a doubt that you can move forward, because God is already there to help you take the next step.*

"But My righteous one will live by faith. And I take no pleasure in the one who shrinks back."

~ Hebrews 10:38

Humble yourselves, therefore, under God's mighty hand, that He may lift you up in due time. Cast all your anxiety on Him because He cares for you.

~ 1 Peter 5:6-7

Great peace have those who love Your law; nothing can make them stumble. I hope for Your salvation, O LORD, and I do Your commandments.

~ Psalm 119:165-166

*Father of Hope, I trust*
*You with my life.*
Amen.

# 34 Do *You* Sometimes Doubt?

It's not unusual for believers to experience doubt every now and again. It sometimes happens that the more we learn about God and other beliefs, the more we start to wonder about our own beliefs. Because we love God with all our heart and all our mind, it is quite normal to struggle with intellectual questions about faith and God.

When you are not sure about a theological issue or have questions, pray and ask God to show you the answers. Seek out a pastor or trusted friend who can help you find the answers.

*Never stop seeking God. Stay on your knees, read His Word, and listen to His Spirit working in your heart. God Himself answers our questions of doubt … when we're ready for it.*

"Who has known the mind of the Lord? Or who has been His counselor?"

~ Romans 11:34

"Then you will know that I am the LORD, for they shall not be ashamed who wait for Me."

~ Isaiah 49:23

Jesus said to the disciples, "Have faith in God. I tell you the truth, you can say to this mountain, 'May you be lifted up and thrown into the sea,' and it will happen. But you must really believe it will happen and have no doubt in your heart."

~ Mark 11:22-23

*Father, help me to cling to You ... even when my heart is filled with doubts.*

Amen.

# 35 After *Winter* ... Comes New Life

Loss is part of life. It happens. And when it does, it is up to us to decide whether we're going to allow it to get us down, or see it as an opportunity for growth.

Jesus chose loss. He gave up His heavenly throne to come to earth; He exchanged His kingship for a simple crib, and happily rested His feet under the tables of tax collectors when He could have dined with royalty. In Gethsemane He chose imprisonment over freedom and finally, He offered up His life. These are the losses that brought us life in Him.

Sometimes God asks us to be people who make sacrifices so that He can give us so much more. He asks that we give Him our soul so that He can save us, that we leave our pain with Him so that He can make us whole again, that we will forgive so that He can forgive us, that we will become less so that His love can become crystal clear in our lives.

*God can use any loss to create something better, more beautiful ... with more eternal worth. When the tough winter times come, remember to think about the beautiful summer He offers you.*

Instead, speaking the truth in love, we will grow to become in every respect the mature body of Him who is the head, that is, Christ.

~ Ephesians 4:15

The LORD will guide you continually, giving you water when you are dry and restoring your strength. You will be like a well-watered garden, like an ever-flowing spring.

~ Isaiah 58:11

He will wipe every tear from their eyes. There will be no more death or mourning or crying or pain, for the old order of things has passed away.

~ Revelation 21:4

*Almighty God, I want to exchange the baggage I've collected all my life for a new vision of the future ... Your vision.*

*Amen.*

# 36 Amidst the Storm
## Say, "*I Believe!*"

Sometimes our circumstances threaten to sink our faith boat. Especially when really bad things happen to really good people and it just makes no sense to us. During such times it is not unusual to hear people say that their faith is starting to shake.

Remember that we are not God. We cannot begin to understand His way of doing things. But, the fact that He is God and we are His people, means that we do not have to understand. Cling only to these truths:

- Jesus loved us so much that He gave us His life. Why would He then find pleasure in our pain?
- The horrible things in this world are not God's fault. It is Satan, trying to tear down every last bit of beauty that is left. And because of sin, we live in a broken world.
- To believe in God does not mean that you will have a life without pain. What it does mean is that you can always know that God's grace will be enough for you no matter the circumstances you face.

*Believe* – *in spite of everything* –
*that God is still in control.*

Surely He took up our pain and bore our suffering, yet we considered Him punished by God, stricken by Him, and afflicted.

~ Isaiah 53:4

Be strong and do not let your hands be weak, for your work shall be rewarded!

~ 2 Chronicles 15:7

God has not given us a spirit of fear and timidity, but of power, love, and self-discipline.

~ 2 Timothy 1:7

*Savior of my life, help me to believe. Help me to know that You will always be the God of love!*
Amen.

# 37 Faith *Is a* Gift

God's love is for all people. Unlike us, God does not just show His love to "good" people. He also doesn't wait to see if we read our Bible regularly, go to church, or faithfully tithe before He offers us His grace.

No, the same sun of salvation that shines on faithful believers also shines on those we think don't deserve it. When our sins leave us feeling dead inside, He comes with arms filled with grace and says, "Here is a free gift for you. Here I am – the One who saved you from death. Accept Me. And go in peace."

Don't allow evil or anybody else to make you doubt God's goodness. Never believe that you aren't worthy of His love or that you first have to fix a few things in your life before you can accept His gift of grace.

*Live life knowing that God – in spite of everything, in spite of who you are and what you've done – shares His love freely with all people.*

Salvation is not a reward for the good things we have done, so none of us can boast about it. For we are God's masterpiece. He has created us anew in Christ Jesus, so we can do the good things He planned for us long ago.

~ Ephesians 2:9-10

Therefore, since we have been justified by faith, we have peace with God through our Lord Jesus Christ.

~ Romans 5:1

The LORD says, "I will rescue those who love Me. I will protect those who trust in My name."

~ Psalm 91:14

*Thank You, Jesus, that I am guaranteed a seat with You in heaven.*

*Amen.*

# 38 God *Works in* Wonderful Ways

How great is our God! And how wonderful that He uses us – broken vessels – in unbelievable ways for His kingdom! Because He is the sovereign and almighty God, He can do anything. God does not need us, and yet He chooses to use us – broken instruments – in His kingdom.

He uses us to change the hearts of other people. With our unique gifts and talents, He can make a difference in other people's lives. And through our words and deeds He makes miracles happen.

Mary was a young, inexperienced woman when God approached her to serve Him. And when He called her, Mary decided to put her own dreams aside and follow God's will. Without hesitance she answered: "I am the Lord's servant, … May your word to me be fulfilled.' Then the angel left her" (Luke 1:38). After this her life changed dramatically and she became known as a blessed woman.

*God wants to use you in a unique way to witness His truth, to share His grace with others and to show His love to others. Will you answer God's call?*

"When you give to someone in need, don't let your left hand know what your right hand is doing. Give your gifts in private, and your Father, who sees everything, will reward you."

~ Matthew 6:3-4

After these things the word of the LORD came to Abram in a vision, saying, "Do not be afraid, Abram. I am your shield, your exceedingly great reward."

~ Genesis 15:1

Older women likewise are to be reverent in behavior, not slanderers or slaves to much wine. They are to teach what is good, and so train the young women to love their husbands and children, to be self-controlled, pure, working at home, kind, and submissive to their own husbands, that the word of God may not be reviled.

~ Titus 2:3-5

*I believe with all my heart that You will work through me in a powerful way today, Lord.*

*Amen.*

# 39 God Is *Your* Hope

Sometimes life can stress us out. We might be asked to do more than we feel we're capable of, we might be forced into a certain direction when we just don't feel up to it, or we might even have to fight for our lives.

Like Saddam Hussein and Martin Luther had to. Both of them had to hide from the most powerful leaders of their time. When Hussein had to hide from Bush and Tony Blair, he hid in a hole. In turn, we read that when the pope and emperor were chasing Martin Luther, he went to work in a castle. There, amidst the threats on his life, he decided to translate the New Testament into German.

How ironic that those who are on the run who don't believe in God bury themselves deeper into a dark pit in times of crisis while a child of God stands stronger than ever.

*Put your hope in God, because when you feel like you can't carry on any more, He will clear the way for you and when you fall, He will catch you.*

Jesus responded, "Why are you afraid? You have so little faith!" Then He got up and rebuked the wind and waves, and suddenly there was a great calm.

~ Matthew 8:26

In all this you greatly rejoice, though now for a little while you may have had to suffer grief in all kinds of trials.

~ 1 Peter 1:6

This is why we work hard and continue to struggle, for our hope is in the living God, who is the Savior of all people and particularly of all believers.

~ 1 Timothy 4:10

*Lord of heaven and earth, still the storm within me and lead me to quiet waters.*

*Amen.*

# 40 Let *Love* Conquer All

**H**as anyone ever knocked the wind out of your sails? You were cruising along when suddenly a strong wind knocked you off course. You wonder how people can treat each other so wrongly.

The question is, what now? Do you hit back, attack, retreat or bottle it up? There is no clear-cut answer, because every situation and every person is unique. Pray that God will give you the self-control you need to step back for a moment, to truly listen and to try to understand.

Ask God to enable you to put yourself in their shoes and to try to see the situation from their perspective. Pray that God will then give you the wisdom you need to react in the right way.

*It's never easy to deal with difficult people and situations. But through the Holy Spirit, it is possible to let love conquer all even in difficult situations.*

He fell on his knees and cried out, "Lord, do not hold this sin against them." When he had said this, he fell asleep.

~ Acts 7:60

God has not given us a spirit of fear and timidity, but of power, love, and self-discipline.

~ 2 Timothy 1:7

Better a patient person than a warrior, one with self-control than one who takes a city.

~ Proverbs 16:32

*Father, take control of my emotions today*
*and guide me in what I need to do.*
*Amen.*

# 41 Positive *People* *Are* Happy People

**W**e can tell ourselves the most outrageous things! That is why we often expect the worst of every situation or person. And then … we are quick to make wrong assumptions. We assume that everything will turn out for the worst, that people think the worst of us and that we are incapable of doing anything, and all this because we've fallen into a habit of looking at the world through negative glasses.

To be positive does not mean ignoring the realities of a situation, rather you live with a pure heart that sees people and situations with the expectation of good. We visualize a positive outcome and work consciously and subconsciously to make it a reality.

Positive people are happy people because they project their positive thoughts onto others. They are happy because they believe that good things will happen, and because they are part of a positive system that makes good things happen. Because they believe the best in everybody, people will do their best to live up to those expectations.

*Live with a heart filled with positive thoughts about what is going to happen, about other people and about yourself. You'll be surprised to see how it all turns out!*

May the God who gives endurance and encouragement give you the same attitude of mind toward each other that Christ Jesus had.

~ Romans 15:5

Finally, brothers, whatever is true, whatever is honorable, whatever is just, whatever is pure, whatever is lovely, whatever is commendable, if there is any excellence, if there is anything worthy of praise, think about these things.

~ Philippians 4:8

Supplement your faith with a generous provision of moral excellence, and moral excellence with knowledge, and knowledge with self-control, and self-control with patient endurance, and patient endurance with godliness, and godliness with brotherly affection, and brotherly affection with love for everyone.

~ 2 Peter 1:6-7

*Lord, I believe in a life of faith, hope and love!*

*Amen.*

# 42 Live *Like a* Winner

**M**aybe you and I will never have the honor of standing on a winner's podium, but that doesn't mean that we can't live like winners.

Once we realize the depth of Christ's love and the implications of our salvation, we can no longer live a humdrum existence. To think that Jesus personally came down to earth to conquer our sins and death so that we could be God's children. How amazing!

Through His grace you can:

- live with a purpose because you know where you're headed
- be confident because He makes you a better person
- work passionately because He is right there to help you
- greet each day with gratitude, knowing that He has already prepared your place in heaven.

*Live today like a winner.*

*Because you are a winner in Jesus Christ.*

Yet in all these things we are more than conquerors through Him who loved us.

~ Romans 8:37

Thanks be to God, who gives us the victory through our Lord Jesus Christ.

~ 1 Corinthians 15:57

I have fought the good fight, I have finished the race, and I have remained faithful. And now the prize awaits me – the crown of righteousness, which the Lord, the righteous Judge, will give me on the day of His return. And the prize is not just for me but for all who eagerly look forward to His appearing.

~ 2 Timothy 4:7-8

*Lord, make me the best me that I can be, determined to achieve my ultimate purpose. I know that You are waiting with my victor's crown at the finish line.*
Amen.

# 43 Dreams *of* Hope

**D**o you ever dream? What are your dreams? Have you ever asked God what you should be dreaming about? Do you live out your dreams?

For once, make time to dream with God. Sit at His feet and ask Him what He had planned for you when He decided to create you. Think about who you want to be, what you want to do and what you want to achieve. Write it down and plan out how you're going to make it happen. Ask God to help you and get started! Success is often a long way off. The quicker you start, the more you'll be able to enjoy the journey.

Inside of you is endless potential, in front of you is wonderful opportunities, and beside you is a God who makes dreams come true.

*Dream big, plan well and do as much as you can.*

Don't envy sinners, but always continue to fear the LORD. You will be rewarded for this; your hope will not be disappointed. My child, listen and be wise: Keep your heart on the right course.

~ Proverbs 23:17-19

Hope deferred makes the heart sick, but a longing fulfilled is a tree of life.

~ Proverbs 13:12

When the LORD brought back the captivity of Zion, we were like those who dream. Then our mouth was filled with laughter, and our tongue with singing. Then they said among the nations, "The LORD has done great things for them." The LORD has done great things for us, and we are glad.

~ Psalm 126:1-3

*Father, help me to see*
*Your dreams for my life*
*and to live to fulfill them.*
*Amen.*

# 44 Make *Your* *Dreams* a Reality

**M**ost people dream about waking up one day and becoming an overnight success. They're halfway right. They will wake up ... because dreams require action.

Dreams are the vision of where we want to be, but action is what turns the dream into a reality. Once you've decided what road you want to travel, you have to be willing to pack your bag, put on your hiking boots and start walking!

Of course there will be times on your journey when you'll feel like giving up, when the road gets too steep and you wonder whether it is even worth it. During such times you have to hang in there and keep going.

*Dreams go hand-in-hand*
*with action. Success means*
*clinging to both. And remember: God wants*
*to help you turn your dreams into a reality.*

She sets about her work vigorously; her arms are strong for her tasks. She sees that her trading is profitable, and her lamp does not go out at night. She is clothed with strength and dignity; she can laugh at the days to come.

~ Proverbs 31:17-18, 25

Take delight in the LORD, and He will give you your heart's desires.

~ Psalm 37:4

"It shall come to pass afterward that I will pour out My Spirit on all flesh; your sons and your daughters shall prophesy, your old men shall dream dreams, your young men shall see visions."

~ Joel 2:28

*Father God, please help me to put my dreams into action.*

*Amen.*

# 45 Dreams *Can* Come True

**K**nowledge means nothing if it isn't used. You can have all the degrees, training and experience in the world, but if you don't use it, it'll sit in your brain gathering dust. How many geniuses never become successful because their exceptional brain power is never used for the benefit of themselves and others?

Then there are many ordinary people who become huge successes in life because they were willing to put their word where their mouth is, to work hard and to persevere. Knowledge is the one thing that does not become second-hand when it is used.

*Your dreams can only become a reality if you are willing to change your attitude, your actions and your work ethic in order to realize them.*

God gives wisdom, knowledge, and joy to those who please Him. But if a sinner becomes wealthy, God takes the wealth away and gives it to those who please Him. This, too, is meaningless – like chasing the wind.

~ Ecclesiastes 2:26

He changes times and seasons; He deposes kings and raises up others. He gives wisdom to the wise and knowledge to the discerning.

~ Daniel 2:21

For the LORD gives wisdom; from His mouth come knowledge and understanding; He stores up sound wisdom for the upright; He is a shield to those who walk uprightly.

~ Proverbs 2:6-7

*Almighty Creator, teach me*
*to truly use what I've learned*
*in life for Your glory.*
*Amen.*

# 46 Do *What* You Love

**D**o you know yourself? Do you know your strengths and gifts, and what you're really good at? Is there something that you enjoy doing so much that you don't want to give it up? If you have the answers to these questions and are doing what you love, chances are you're already successful.

Successful people do what they love. The flip side is also true: Few people truly become successful in the things they don't like to do. Gallup has a great test that you can complete to figure out what your strengths and talents are – *Now, Discover Your Strength*. It could possibly help you to realize your unique abilities and to start using them.

Know who you are. You can only know what you want to achieve once you've learned who you are.

*Your Creator wants you to discover and live out your true potential. Find out what makes your heart sing. Do it passionately and with everything you've got!*

In His grace, God has given us different gifts for doing certain things well. So if God has given you the ability to prophesy, speak out with as much faith as God has given you.

~ Romans 12:6

How joyful are those who fear the Lord – all who follow His ways! You will enjoy the fruit of your labor. How joyful and prosperous you will be!

~ Psalm 128:1-2

*Lord, help me to discover my strengths, to develop them and to fulfill my life's purpose.*

*Amen.*

# 47 God *Loves* You

**G**od in His endless love only wants what's best for you, just like you want for your kids. Now we all know that sometimes "the best" thing for our kids is to discipline them and to prepare them as best we can for life.

Because God loves you so much, He will allow certain things to happen in your life and you might experience hardships. Of course these painful and difficult times are never fun and we might be left wondering why God would allow something like that to happen. No child has ever seen the discipline they receive from their parents as an honor. God also doesn't expect us to be happy when we're having a difficult time. He knows us, understands us and knows that trials are anything but fun.

*Yet nothing can happen to you without the Father's consent. Cling to the hope that no pain or difficulty will come your way without the grace of God!*

For whom the LORD loves He corrects, just as a father the son in whom he delights.

~ Proverbs 3:12

This is love: not that we loved God, but that He loved us and sent His Son as an atoning sacrifice for our sins.

~ 1 John 4:10

"I lavish unfailing love for a thousand generations on those who love Me and obey My commands."

~ Exodus 20:6

*Thank You, Father, that You love me enough to discipline me and help me to grow.*

*Amen.*

# 48 *Clean* Laundry

We often hide what is in our hearts with a firm word or two. In this way, we fool each other with kind words when really we're thinking the complete opposite. And then, one day, we explode and shoot out all those bottled-up thoughts at someone … this causes big and unnecessary damage. The fact is, we can't keep the dirty laundry in our hearts bottled up for very long. Sooner or later our true colors will shine through.

Solomon knew what he was talking about when he said that the most important foundation of wisdom is what goes on in our heart. We have to purify our heart by surrendering it to the Spirit of God each and every day. He is the only One who can take out the dirty laundry of our heart, wash it and neatly put it back where it belongs. Only He can wash out the blemishes that stain our lives and replace it with God's love.

*Pray that the Holy Spirit will purify your heart so that you will think differently about other people, believe the best in everyone and be pure in your love for others.*

Guard your heart above all else, for it determines the course of your life. Avoid all perverse talk; stay away from corrupt speech.

~ Proverbs 4:23-24

Restore to me the joy of Your salvation and grant me a willing spirit, to sustain me.

~ Psalm 51:12

Run from anything that stimulates youthful lusts. Instead, pursue righteous living, faithfulness, love, and peace. Enjoy the companionship of those who call on the Lord with pure hearts.

~ 2 Timothy 2:22

*Spirit of God, purify my heart and fill it with all of You.*

*Amen.*

# 49 Focus on the Light

**M**aybe you are struggling with a few things and life is just not making sense for you right now. Maybe the day feels like an impossible mountain you have to climb, or life feels hopeless, pointless and meaningless to you.

This is exactly the time you need to praise God, to be still and focus your thoughts on Him. Because praise does not change God; praise changes our hearts. When you and I praise our heavenly Father with all our heart and soul, thanking Him and honoring Him, something happens inside us. Our focus is shifted from earthly things to that of heaven and the things we struggle with become small in light of the eternal.

When we enter the throne room of God with a humble spirit and praise Him for what He does for us and who He is, there is no way we can walk out untouched. Because it is then that His light shines into every area of our lives and we start thinking and feeling differently about things.

*Focus on the Lord for a few minutes.*
*Tell Him why you love Him so much.*

While I live I will praise the LORD; I will sing praises to my God while I have my being.

~ Psalm 146:2

Praise be to the God and Father of our Lord Jesus Christ, who has blessed us in the heavenly realms with every spiritual blessing in Christ.

~ Ephesians 1:3

For with You is the fountain of life; in Your light we see light.

~ Psalm 36:9

*Lord, I honor and praise You. I love You so much. I bring You all the glory for being my loving Father.*

*Amen.*

# 50 A Ripple *Effect* of Hope

Every time someone stands up for what he believes in, or fights for an ideal or for someone else, it sends a rippling effect of hope through the world.

Maybe you are wondering how you too can give someone a little bit of hope. Because, just like you, everyone on earth is trying to survive in their small world and longing to experience a life of happiness and contentment. Once we realize this, we will start to see other people differently, to think about them differently. It is then that we realize that our friends, family, colleagues, the cashier, the person in front of you in the queue, are all looking for hope.

And you, in your own unique way, have the ability to encourage them and give them the hope they long for. It's not always the big things that cause a ripple effect of hope, because hope can sometimes come in the shape of a spontaneous smile, an encouraging word, positive comments and true caring love.

*You can give someone the hope they need today by just going out and living God's love.*

I also pray that you will understand the incredible greatness of God's power for us who believe Him.

~ Ephesians 1:19

Therefore encourage one another and build each other up, just as in fact you are doing.

~ 1 Thessalonians 5:11

Rejoice with those who rejoice, weep with those who weep.

~ Romans 12:15

*Lord, I want to spread hope.*
*I want to cause a ripple*
*effect in my world today.*
*Amen.*

# 51 The Voice
## *of* Hope

It was an ordinary dove that played a big role in Noah's life. Noah needed to know when it was safe to open up the ark's door and let everyone out, so he sent out a dove three times to find the answer he was looking for.

The first time, the dove turned around and came back because he couldn't find a dry place to perch amid the endless stretch of water. The second time the dove returned with an olive branch of hope. A week later this small branch of hope became a reality when the dove found its new home among the branches of a tree. Noah knew that it was almost time.

The godly Dove – the Spirit of God – still speaks to us today:

- Sometimes He says, "Be patient. When the right time comes, you'll find your answer."
- At other times He whispers, "I want to bless you with the olive branches of life. Find rest where you are right now."
- And then there are times when the Holy Spirit gives us the green light: "Do what I ask of you. The time has come."

*What is the* Holy Spirit
*saying to you today?*

So he waited yet another seven days and sent out the dove, which did not return again to him anymore.

~ Genesis 8:12

If any of you lacks wisdom, you should ask God, who gives generously to all without finding fault, and it will be given to you.

~ James 1:5

"When the Spirit of truth comes, He will guide you into all truth. He will not speak on His own but will tell you what He has heard. He will tell you about the future."

~ John 16:13

*Speak, Lord, I'm listening.*

*I will do what You tell me to do.*

*Amen.*

# 52 Obedience *Brings* Blessing

The Bible does not beat about the bush when it comes to obedience. God doesn't like it when we are disobedient because He knows how it influences us and the rest of the world in a negative way. He tells us that obedience will result in many blessings. Blessings in the form of fulfillment, inner peace, contentment and love.

Remember today, you never have to doubt how much God loves you – even when you are disobedient. But remember also that by being disobedient, we can miss out on the blessings and favor God has planned for us.

Declare again today your dependence, obedience and willingness to follow the God who only has the best things planned for you. He wants to bless you.

*Pray this prayer right now:*

*I love You,*

*Lord, and therefore I want to do whatever*
*You ask of me and follow in Your steps. Amen.*

"I will make you like My signet ring, for I have chosen you," declares the LORD Almighty.

~ Haggai 2:23

"If you love Me, obey My commandments."

~ John 14:15

You will receive this blessing if you are careful to obey all the commands of the LORD your God that I am giving you today. The LORD your God will bless you as He has promised. You will lend money to many nations but will never need to borrow. You will rule many nations, but they will not rule over you.

~ Deuteronomy 15:5-6

*Thank You, Bridegroom of my heart,*
*that I am Your bride and that You want to*
*shower me with Your blessings of love.*

*Amen.*

# 53 His Rainbow of Promises

**R**ainbows have a way of bringing people to a stand-still. Because, apart from the beauty and wonder of this seven-color creation, it reminds us that God created it as a sign of His unshakable promises of faithfulness to us.

History has proven that God has kept every promise He has made … even that His own Son had to die. God is serious about His promises of life and salvation, but He is also faithful in the small things in our lives. God doesn't just hear you when you pray for guidance, strength and wisdom, He promises to be with you every step of the way.

Hope is the unshakable certainty that God's promises will come true – founded on the realities of life, death and the resurrection of Jesus Christ.

*The next time you see God's rainbow of grace, remember that He wants to bless His children – including you.*

"I have set My rainbow in the clouds, and it will be the sign of the covenant between Me and the earth. Whenever I bring clouds over the earth and the rainbow appears in the clouds, I will remember My covenant between Me and you and all living creatures of every kind. Never again will the waters become a flood to destroy all life."

~ Genesis 9:13-15

He made heaven and earth, the sea, and everything in them. He keeps every promise forever.

~ Psalm 146:6

He is the Lord our God. His justice is seen throughout the land. He always stands by His covenant – the commitment He made to a thousand generations.

~ Psalm 105:7-8

*Thank You, Lord, that You are faithful even in the smallest details of my life.*
*Amen.*

# 54 A Rainbow of Grace

There is a legend of a wealthy king who suffered from severe depression. Someone told the king that he would be healed if only he wore the coat of a very happy man. Immediately he sent out his servants to find such a man. After searching for a long time, they finally found a man who believed that he was the happiest man in the world. The only problem was … he was too poor to own a coat.

Our heavenly Father puts thousands of rainbows in our lives every day. Our world is filled to the brim with colorful snippets of blessing. Just think of a good night's rest or the fact that your body – even while you are sleeping – keeps functioning. Or that you are healthy, can work, have food to eat … people to love … and know the God who is faithful to you unto death.

Let us experience fully the wonderful grace in our lives: Let's see, hear, smell, taste and feel with new wonder how the drops of God's grace fall on us today.

*Experience and accept the beautiful rainbows of grace God blesses us with every day.*

The LORD watches over you – the LORD is your shade at your right hand; the sun will not harm you by day, nor the moon by night. The LORD will keep you from all harm – He will watch over your life; the LORD will watch over your coming and going both now and forevermore.

~ Psalm 121:5-8

For the LORD God is a sun and shield; the LORD will give grace and glory; no good thing will He withhold from those who walk uprightly. O LORD of hosts, blessed is the man who trusts in You!

~ Psalm 84:11-12

When I felt secure, I said, "I will never be shaken."

~ Psalm 30:6

*God of Grace, I praise You for every rainbow of blessing that You put in my life. Open my eyes to its beauty.*

*Amen.*

# 55 A Star of Hope

**R**esearch shows that women radiate some kind of "good feeling" hormones when they spend time with their inner circle of friends. Isn't it wonderful that our Father gives us friends? True friends know how much friendship is worth. That is why they will always …

- keep each other's secrets
- accept each other and forgive one another
- make time to get to know each other better, and
- put energy and effort into the relationship.

Don't allow your busy schedule, or anything else for that matter, to come between you and your friends. You need them and they need you. God wants you to enjoy the wonder of true friendship.

*True friendship is like a bright star on a dark night: It always gives hope. It is like ice water on a hot summer's day: It quenches your thirst. It's a masterpiece painted by two hearts that should be cherished and taken care of.*

One who has unreliable friends soon comes to ruin, but there is a friend who sticks closer than a brother.

~ Proverbs 18:24

A friend loves at all times, and a brother is born for adversity.

~ Proverbs 17:17

It is right for me to feel this way about all of you, since I have you in my heart and, whether I am in chains or defending and confirming the gospel, all of you share in God's grace with me. God can testify how I long for all of you with the affection of Christ Jesus.

~ Philippians 1:7-8

The heartfelt counsel of a friend is as sweet as perfume and incense.

~ Proverbs 27:9

*Lord, make me a true, caring friend whom other people can trust with their hearts.*

*Amen.*

# 56 Prayer *Is an* Act of Faith

**S**ometimes we wonder about the future. So many things happen, or don't happen, that leave us feeling worried and upset in the world today.

Thousands of years ago, the Israelites found themselves in an even more stressful situation. A big group of Judeans had been captured and taken to Babylon. And not many of them still faithfully served God. It was during that hopeless time that God, beyond logical reasoning, decided to tell Jeremiah to buy a piece of land. No one in their right mind would have done that, and yet … Jeremiah did exactly what God had asked of him. He believed that God was a God of the impossible. He was able to look past his own circumstances because he knew the Lord was in control.

Prayer is an act of faith, as Jeremiah also realized. It is looking beyond your own situation and seeing the God of the future, calling out to Him and doing what He tells you to do without hesitation.

*Today, look past all the things that upset you and pray to the God who is in control. He has the power to change you and everything else around you.*

You have said to me, O Lord GOD, "Buy the field for money, and take witnesses"! – yet the city has been given into the hand of the Chaldeans.

~ Jeremiah 32:25

Listen to my cry for help, my King and my God, for I pray to no one but You. Listen to my voice in the morning, LORD. Each morning I bring my requests to You and wait expectantly.

~ Psalm 5:2-3

"Then you will call upon Me and go and pray to Me, and I will listen to you. And you will seek Me and find Me, when you search for Me with all your heart."

~ Jeremiah 29:12-13

*Father God, help me to look beyond my current situation ... and to put my hope in You. I want to believe with all my heart!*

Amen.

# 57 Light *and* Hope

It sometimes feels like we are experiencing crucifixion Friday. Yes, we wonder whether God even sees the brokenness and confusion in this world, and we even doubt if He is still in control.

Why else would we read in the media about so much pain, corruption and suffering happening all around us? In times like these, we should remember that after that dark Friday when our Savior died, Sunday came. A Sunday on which Jesus rose from the dead and comforted His friends at the grave, telling them not to be afraid.

God's grace does not end during our darkest hours. It goes with us through the dark tunnel until we can see the light and feel the hope in our hearts. Jesus conquered death 2,000 years ago to bring us the Light of life. And He is still doing it today. Even in this dark, broken age, He is the Light.

*During the dark hours of your life, cling*

*to the knowledge that there will always*

*be a Sunday of Light*

*after the darkness of Friday because*

*the Living Father is always with us.*

Then Jesus said to them, "Do not be afraid. Go and tell My brothers to go to Galilee; there they will see Me."

~ Matthew 28:10

Then this message came to Jeremiah from the LORD: "I am the LORD, the God of all the peoples of the world. Is anything too hard for Me?"

~ Jeremiah 32:26-27

But now, Lord, what do I look for? My hope is in you. Save me from all my transgressions; do not make me the scorn of fools.

~ Psalm 39:7-8

Yea, though I walk through the valley of the shadow of death, I will fear no evil; for You are with me; Your rod and Your staff, they comfort me.

~ Psalm 23:4

*Thank You, Father, for never abandoning nor forsaking me.*
*Amen.*

# 58 *going*
# Nowhere Slowly

Have you ever experienced days when it feels like you're stuck in a bubble, going nowhere slowly? You might have left solid ground to jump to another point, but you haven't landed yet.

You desperately try to set foot on solid ground, floundering around in the air, but now you're not so sure if you'll even be able to make the jump. Here, in the unknown and unfamiliar place of floating around, it can get quite lonely.

We all experience such times in our lives when it feels like the rug has been pulled from under our feet. It is quite easy to panic, feel scared or uncertain of your footing. But remember, God is present in the voids of our lives. He holds out His hand to catch us when we fall. He carries us to safety so that we can know that we are safe in His arms.

*Keep your eyes, your expectations and your hope focused on God who hides you safely under His wings during the certain and not-so-certain times.*

God is my strong fortress, and He makes my way perfect. He makes me as surefooted as a deer, enabling me to stand on mountain heights.

~ 2 Samuel 22:33-34

The LORD is my rock, my fortress and my deliverer; my God is my rock, in whom I take refuge, my shield and the horn of my salvation, my stronghold.

~ Psalm 18:2

He will not let your foot be moved; He who keeps you will not slumber. The LORD will keep you from all evil; He will keep your life.

~ Psalm 121:3, 7

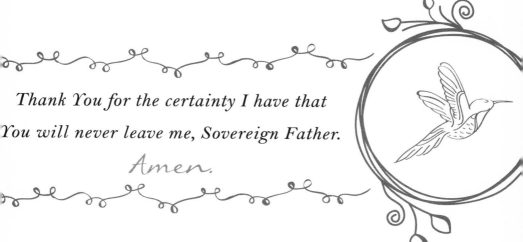

*Thank You for the certainty I have that You will never leave me, Sovereign Father.*

Amen.

# 59 When Discouraged ... He Is There

**D**o you sometimes feel discouraged by your own emotions? Why is it that our female hearts so easily tumble and fall? The one day we feel fine: we feel good about ourselves, our world and the people around us. The next moment we find ourselves flat-faced on the ground. Everyone and everything around us seem like one big mountain. Worst of all, it is during such times that we seem to look worse too! It is then that we should remember:

- God doesn't just love us when we feel good about ourselves, are being productive and go out into the world with a smile on our faces. He is the Father of those who struggle to stay on their feet, and those who find it impossible to see the light.
- God also doesn't look over our shoulders in the mirror to see how good we look before He decides to love us or not. He looks past our make-up. He loves our souls.
- God never changes. He doesn't love us less one day and more the next.

*Thank God that His love for you always stays the same – no matter how you feel.*

Jesus Christ is the same yesterday and today and forever.

~ Hebrews 13:8

Give thanks to the LORD, for He is good. His love endures forever.

~ Psalm 136:1

For the LORD is good; His mercy is everlasting, and His truth endures to all generations.

~ Psalm 100:5

*Father, thank You that Your love for me is not determined by my roller coaster of emotions.*

Amen.

# 60 The *Beauty* of Hope

**W**hen Paul and Silas were thrown in prison, they had more than enough reason to be discouraged and feel sorry for themselves. But the two men chose differently. They chose to sing songs of praise to God, to worship Him … despite the pain in their bodies and the darkness of their prison cell.

Later on, we read about the miracle that took place in Acts 16. An earthquake broke open the cell doors, and the chains around their ankles fell to the ground. Even more amazing is that the prison guards came to faith and later helped to bandage the prisoners' wounds. God simply turned their situation around.

You always have a choice – even when it feels like the prison doors of life are shut right in your face. You can choose whether you are going to wallow in self-pity and discouragement, or whether you are going to believe, and keep hoping. And continue to praise the Lord.

*Choose to live in the beauty of hope even when you don't feel like it.*

About midnight Paul and Silas were praying and singing hymns to God, and the other prisoners were listening to them.

~ Acts 16:25

When anxiety was great within me, Your consolation brought me joy.

~ Psalm 94:19

I will bless the LORD who has given me counsel; my heart also instructs me in the night seasons. I have set the LORD always before me; because He is at my right hand I shall not be moved. Therefore my heart is glad, and my glory rejoices; my flesh also will rest in hope.

~ Psalm 16:7-9

*Sovereign God, teach me to trust You in everything and to know that You are always in control.*

*Amen.*

# 61 God *Wants to* Surprise You

**J**esus Christ came to earth to ensure that we would one day enter into a new and wonderful world. How great to be able to look forward to eternal life!

But our heavenly Father also wants us to live like new people on earth who realize that His grace is new every morning. Because of this and in spite of everything that happened yesterday and the day before, you can give your heart to God. Ask Him now and every new morning to:

- forgive your sins and cleanse your guilt-ridden heart
- stitch every torn piece of your life back together with His hope
- wipe away your hurt and pain with His comfort
- and color your washed up dreams with new passion.

*God wants to be good to you today. You can look forward to a new day filled with His grace; a day which He will use to surprise you.*

The LORD is gracious and righteous; our God is full of compassion. Return to your rest, my soul, for the LORD has been good to you.

~ Psalm 116:5, 7

Because of the LORD's great love we are not consumed, for His compassions never fail. They are new every morning; great is Your faithfulness.

~ Lamentations 3:22-23

Let integrity and uprightness preserve me, for I wait for You.

~ Psalm 25:21

*Lord, I look forward to following Your great plan for me today.*
*Amen.*

# 62 God Is Faithful

**O**ptimism is believing in possibilities; hope is believing in what God has already done, and can do again. People disappoint people. Sometimes they do it subconsciously, at other times without thinking and sometimes it just happens because of weakness.

The fact is, God's faithfulness is unfailing and unshakable … even unto death. When you doubt, go through your Bible and you'll find all the different ways in which God held His children safe. Also think back on all the times He carried you through the drift, strengthened you and gave you the answers you sought.

Also know that God, who loves you with all His heart, wants only what's best for you. Believe that you can achieve anything, overcome any difficulty and travel any road successfully with Him by your side.

*Take God at His word when you read in the Bible: He is faithful to keep His promises.*

Let us hold unswervingly to the hope we profess, for He who promised is faithful.

~ Hebrews 10:23

But the Lord is faithful; He will strengthen you and guard you from the evil one. May the Lord lead your hearts into a full understanding and expression of the love of God and the patient endurance that comes from Christ.

~ 2 Thessalonians 3:3, 5

The LORD is righteous in all His ways, gracious in all His works. The LORD is near to all who call upon Him, to all who call upon Him in truth. He will fulfill the desire of those who fear Him; He also will hear their cry and save them. The LORD preserves all who love Him, but all the wicked He will destroy.

~ Psalm 145:17-20

*I believe and trust in You with all my heart.*

*Amen.*

# 63 This *Too* Shall Pass

When we find ourselves in the middle of a crisis, it can often feel like the world stands still. It's like nothing else matters except our broken, painful moments. And after much struggle, it seems like there will never be an end to it. When we feel like this, it's a good idea to read about David who wrote many psalms on feelings just like these.

He found himself more than once in a dark pit of discouragement. And yet, it is so encouraging when we read where he says, "My soul is downcast within me; therefore I will remember You. Deep calls to deep in the roar of Your waterfalls; all Your waves and breakers have swept over me" (Ps. 42:6-7).

My dear friend, remember that times of crises will pass. Yes, soon you'll look back and know: God was faithful even when your world seemed to be falling apart.

*There is an end to everything – except God's unfailing love. Go out and live your life, encouraged by this bit of wisdom.*

Therefore we will not fear, though the earth give way and the mountains fall into the heart of the sea, though its waters roar and foam and the mountains quake with their surging. Come and see what the LORD has done, the desolations He has brought on the earth.

~ Psalm 46:2-3, 8

O my Strength, to You I sing praises, for You, O God, are my refuge, the God who shows me unfailing love.

~ Psalm 59:17-18

We wait in hope for the LORD; He is our help and our shield. In Him our hearts rejoice, for we trust in His holy name. May Your unfailing love be with us, LORD, even as we put our hope in You.

~ Psalm 33:20-22

*Thank You, Father God,*
*that I can put my hope,*
*expectations and vision*
*for a better future*
*in Your hands.*

# 64 Blessed *Hope*

As broken people we are easily overcome by uncertainty. We get scared quickly. All day and every day things happen around us that we have no control over. When in doubt, or when we feel uncertain and scared, read all the stories about God's faithfulness in His Word. Stories like that of Joshua:

- Without any bloodshed, God gave the city of Jericho into his hands (see Josh. 6).
- When Joshua and his men needed the sun to shine a little longer in order to defeat the mighty city of Gibbon, God made the sun stand still (see Josh. 10).
- In many ways, God led Joshua through impossible situations (see Josh. 6).

The Bible is filled with tons of stories about how God strengthened ordinary people who were scared, blessed them with miracles and gave them hope. All that was needed was faith, obedience and a willingness to do what God asked of them.

*When God is with you,*
*you need not fear.*

"Do not be afraid of them," the Lᴏʀᴅ said to Joshua, "for I have given you victory over them. Not a single one of them will be able to stand up to you."

~ Joshua 10:8

Be strong and courageous. Do not be afraid or terrified because of them, for the Lᴏʀᴅ your God goes with you; He will never leave you nor forsake you.

~ Deuteronomy 31:6

"Have I not commanded you? Be strong and of good courage; do not be afraid, nor be dismayed, for the Lᴏʀᴅ your God is with you wherever you go."

~ Joshua 1:9

*Because of You I am not*
*afraid, Lord. You are in control.*

*Amen.*

# 65 *Embrace* God's Promises

The more you read God's Word, apply His truths to your life and make the wonders of the Bible your own, the more you will want to get to know Him better. The closer you draw to Him, the more you'll enjoy being in His presence. That is why it is so important to read His Word and truly make His message your own. Apply the following guidelines when you read the Bible:

- Ask yourself what is God trying to tell me here? What is God really asking?
- Decide that you want to do what He asks because, as a child of God, this is how you should be living.
- Pray that God will help you follow His guidelines.
- Make the Scriptures your own. Speak it and believe that you are already a victor through the power of the Holy Spirit and that you already live the way God wants you to. Embrace God's promises of faithfulness, hope and comfort, and know that He will always keep His promises.

*God still speaks to His children through His unchanging truths. Embrace them, make them your own and live in His wonderful light.*

Send me Your light and Your faithful care, let them lead me; let them bring me to Your holy mountain, to the place where You dwell.

~ Psalm 43:3

Every word of God is flawless; He is a shield to those who take refuge in Him.

~ Proverbs 30:5

In the beginning was the Word, and the Word was with God, and the Word was God. He was with God in the beginning. Through Him all things were made; without Him nothing was made that has been made.

~ John 1:1-3

*Heavenly Father, let Your truths and love shine through powerfully in my life today.*

*Amen.*

# 66 Live a Passionate Life

There have been many times that I felt as if I've angered or disappointed God. That is why I am so grateful that my God – our God – is not human. Because no human being can forgive and accept somebody so many times and still love them so much.

There truly is no other father quite like our heavenly Father. That is why we can live in freedom. No matter where we are on our faith journey, every morning we can start afresh with new courage and hope.

When we place yesterday's baggage at the cross of forgiveness in sincere repentance, we can begin our journey of freedom. And because we are free, we can live life passionately.

*Do you live every day as if it's your last? Do you experience God's grace in everything you do? Praise the Lord, because there is none like Him!*

Who is a God like You, who pardons sin and forgives the transgression of the remnant of His inheritance? You do not stay angry forever but delight to show mercy.

~ Micah 7:18

All glory to Him who loves us and has freed us from our sins by shedding His blood for us. He has made us a Kingdom of priests for God His Father. All glory and power to Him forever and ever!

~ Revelation 1:5-6

Blessed are those whose ways are blameless, who walk according to the law of the LORD. Blessed are those who keep His statutes and seek Him with all their heart – they do no wrong but follow His ways.

~ Psalm 119:1-3

*I praise You, Father God,*
*for Your unfailing love*
*and grace in my life.*
Amen.

# 67 Worth *More Than* Sparrows

Sparrows are not the most beautiful birds or the most expensive. When Jesus walked the earth, you could have bought two sparrows for a penny. Today we barely even notice these birds. But in Matthew 10:29, Jesus says, "Are not two sparrows sold for a penny? Yet not one of them will fall to the ground outside your Father's care." If God cares so much for one small bird, how can you doubt His incredible love and care for you?

If you are going through a difficult time in your life and you're wondering whether God understands your deepest thoughts, longings, and pain, listen when He tells you today: "The very hairs of your head are all numbered. Do not fear therefore; you are of more value than many sparrows" (Matt. 10:30-31).

It is believed that we lose approximately 90 hairs every day. Can you imagine that God even knows about every single one of them? Do you realize just how important you are to Him and how much He truly loves you?

*Close your eyes and allow God to cover you with His love and tell you, "You are worth so much more than a sparrow, My dearly beloved child."*

Are not two sparrows sold for a penny? Yet not one of them will fall to the ground outside your Father's care. And even the very hairs of your head are all numbered.

~ Matthew 10:29-30

God showed His great love for us by sending Christ to die for us while we were still sinners.

~ Romans 5:8

"Because you are precious in My eyes, and honored, and I love you, I give ... peoples in exchange for your life."

~ Isaiah 43:4

*Thank You, Father, that You*
*cover me safely in Your loving arms.*

*Amen.*

# 68 A Refuge for the Lost

Children of God never need to feel hopeless. Yet, we have days when we mess up and feel sorry for ourselves, perhaps even contemplating giving up all together. There can even come a time when you'll wonder whether your sins aren't too many for God's grace to cover this time round.

The message of the Gospel is that God came to save the lost. He is the Shepherd who would temporarily leave His 99 sheep to go and look for the one sheep that got lost. And when you are the one who is lost, you can know with certainty that He wants you back – no matter what the reasons were for you getting lost in the first place. He will look for you, call you back to Him and guide you safely back to the flock.

Do you hear Him calling you today? Is the uncertainty or discomfort you feel perhaps the Holy Spirit asking you to return home? And do you realize that He does it because He loves you so very much?

*Find comfort in knowing that Jesus came to save the lost. Kneel before Him, because that is where you belong.*

"At that time I will plant a crop of Israelites and raise them for Myself. I will show love to those I called 'Not loved.' And to those I called 'Not My people,' I will say, 'Now you are My people.' And they will reply, 'You are our God!'"

~ Hosea 2:23

"I have swept away your offenses like a cloud, your sins like the morning mist. Return to Me, for I have redeemed you."

~ Isaiah 44:22

He also brought me up out of a horrible pit, out of the miry clay, and set my feet upon a rock, and established my steps. He has put a new song in my mouth – praise to our God; many will see it and fear, and will trust in the LORD. Blessed is that man who makes the LORD his trust, and does not respect the proud, nor such as turn aside to lies.

~ Psalm 40:2-4

*Loving Father, I come to You just*
*as I am … please take my heart.*
*Amen.*

# 69 Make *Dreams* Come True

We all dream about being successful. Everyone has some kind of desire to be someone important or achieve something great. But dreams will become nothing more than just dreams if we aren't willing to work hard at making them a reality.

When we look at successful people, it is easy to think that they got lucky or that things just fell in place for them. The opposite is in fact true. All successful people took one step at a time and approached the finish line themselves. They:

- always had a clear vision of where they were heading,
- felt passionate about what they were doing,
- were prepared to work hard, and
- persevered even when everyone else had given up.

*You can also make your dreams come true if you are willing to put your heart and soul into making it a reality.*

Work willingly at whatever you do, as though you were working for the Lord rather than for people.

~ Colossians 3:23

If the ax is dull, and one does not sharpen the edge, then he must use more strength; but wisdom brings success.

~ Ecclesiastes 10:10

Commit to the Lord whatever you do, and He will establish your plans.

~ Proverbs 16:3

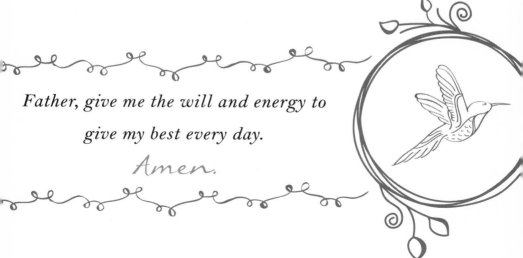

*Father, give me the will and energy to give my best every day.*

*Amen.*

# 70 His Grace Is Enough

When life knocks you down and you struggle to get up again and mend your broken heart, you secretly hope that it would all just disappear.

Paul also felt this way when he asked God three times to take his pain away. The thorn in his side had been too much for him to bear for a long time. God heard his cry and understood his pain, but said, "No." Yet it is not a "No" without comfort. God promised him: "My grace is enough for you."

This same gracious God loves you just as much! That is why He promises you that He will never send anything your way that you can't handle. For every hurt, He'll send His loving salve; for every cut, He'll send more than enough bandages of grace.

You might feel at times that His grace is only just enough. But He knows what you can handle and His grace will be enough for you!

*Sometimes God allows us to travel painful and difficult roads so that He can shower us with grace for our journey.*

"My grace is sufficient for you, for My power is made perfect in weakness."

~ 2 Corinthians 12:9

Don't tear your clothing in your grief, but tear your hearts instead. Return to the LORD your God, for He is merciful and compassionate, slow to get angry and filled with unfailing love. He is eager to relent and not punish.

~ Joel 2:13

The LORD is compassionate and gracious, slow to anger, abounding in love. He will not always accuse, nor will He harbor His anger forever; He does not treat us as our sins deserve or repay us according to our iniquities. For as high as the heavens are above the earth, so great is His love for those who fear Him.

~ Psalm 103:8-11

*Lord, thank You for giving me enough of everything: Your love, support and especially grace.*

*Amen.*

# 71 Close to *His* Heart

When you get bad news, fall ill, or when the worst happens, it is normal to wonder, *How am I going to survive? Is God really with me? Do I even have a tomorrow to hope for?* The answer to all of these questions is "Yes!" God, your faithful Father, holds your future in His hands. And especially at this point, He is closer to you than ever before.

Even when we're scared and plagued by doubts, God is still with His children. It might be that He, in His omniscience, decided not to take your pain away because He has something greater planned for you. But in your hour of need, He remains your faithful and loving Father – the One who will not allow a single hair on your head to fall without Him knowing about it. In your heartache, the Holy Spirit will comfort you.

When you can no longer see the light, when words fail you and you feel hopeless in your pain, His Word is there to strengthen you.

*When you feel like you can't hold on*

*any more, know that He is holding you*

*ever close to His heart.*

Those who look to Him are radiant; their faces are never covered with shame. This poor man called, and the LORD heard him; He saved him out of all his troubles.

~ Psalm 34:5-6

Do not hide Your face from me; do not turn Your servant away in anger; You have been my help; do not leave me nor forsake me, O God of my salvation. When my father and my mother forsake me, then the LORD will take care of me.

~ Psalm 27:9-10

Though they stumble, they will never fall, for the LORD holds them by the hand.

~ Psalm 37:24

*Father, Son and Holy Spirit, hold me close.*

*Amen.*

# 72 Trials *Build* Character

People who know suffering are changed by it, and are left different – for the better. They are calmer, wiser and have more depth of character. They have a better understanding, empathy and sympathy for others.

Those who have suffered are normally also those who know how to give. Maybe it's because they've learned through their own uphill battles to turn away from themselves and focus on others more … to recognize the tired feet of fellow travelers.

God doesn't send trials our way for no reason. He allows it so that we can better understand other people's circumstances and needs and in so doing can help them through it. You will find that when you have gone through a difficult and painful situation, it is much easier to show sympathy, understanding and encouragement to others going through the same struggle. And what a blessing that is!

Ask God to give you a caring heart – someone whose heart is moved by other people's hurt and pain. Be someone to help others get through it.

*Make difficult times worth going through. For your sake and for others.*

We can rejoice, too, when we run into problems and trials, for we know that they help us develop endurance. And endurance develops strength of character, and character strengthens our confident hope of salvation. And this hope will not lead to disappointment. For we know how dearly God loves us, because He has given us the Holy Spirit to fill our hearts with His love.

~ Romans 5:3-5

Therefore encourage one another and build each other up, just as in fact you are doing.

~ 1 Thessalonians 5:11

Blessed be the God and Father of our Lord Jesus Christ, the Father of mercies and God of all comfort, who comforts us in all our affliction, so that we may be able to comfort those who are in any affliction, with the comfort with which we ourselves are comforted by God.

~ 2 Corinthians 1:3-4

*Loving Father, teach me
to use my own pain to help
other people with theirs.*
*Amen.*

# 73 *Look* Up!

Sometimes we can lose perspective on life because we spend too much time looking down and not enough time looking up. Then we easily lose hope.

Today, the Father is calling you by name and saying to you: "Look up. Look up and see Me. See the tender care in My eyes, My hand reaching out to you … see the hope I offer you."

Your heavenly Father knows your circumstances, He understands your heart, feels your pain and knows what is best for you. At the right time and in His own way He will give you the answers, wisdom and show you the way out. He'll strengthen you when you're weak, guide you when you need answers and comfort, and He will bless you.

Remember that …

- God hears your cry for help and sees your discouraged heart.
- He is there to hold you, support you and guide you in the way you should go.
- God's vision is so much wider and goes so much deeper than ours – trust Him.

*Look up to God with renewed hope. With Him all things are possible.*

I lift up my eyes to the mountains – where does my help come from? My help comes from the LORD, the Maker of heaven and earth. The LORD will keep you from all harm – He will watch over your life; the LORD will watch over your coming and going both now and forevermore.

~ Psalm 121:1-2, 7-8

May Your unfailing love be my comfort, according to Your promise to Your servant. Let Your compassion come to me that I may live, for Your law is my delight.

~ Psalm 119:76-77

Then as Elijah lay and slept under a broom tree, suddenly an angel touched him, and said to him, "Arise and eat." Then he looked, and there by his head was a cake baked on coals, and a jar of water. So he ate and drank, and lay down again.

~ 1 Kings 19:5-6

*Thank You, God, that You know my future. You know all about me. Your plans for me are all for good.*

Amen.

# 74 Glasses of Hope

**S**ometimes it becomes really difficult to see the positive side of life. A proven way to get rid of our "What else could possibly go wrong" and a "What horrible thing is going to happen next" attitude, is to rather look at the world through God's eyes.

Our Father always sees …

- the good and beautiful in others,
- the positive side of life,
- that anything is possible,
- life from an eternal perspective.

Give all your worries to God today – without taking anything back. Expect good – without looking for the negative. Believe the best about others – without judging them. In this way you will see a ray of sunshine between the clouds, happiness in the midst of pain and laugh through your tears.

*Look at the world through godly glasses of faith, hope and love.*

Count it all joy, my brothers, when you meet trials of various kinds, for you know that the testing of your faith produces steadfastness.

~ James 1:2-3

You make known to me the path of life; in Your presence there is fullness of joy; at Your right hand are pleasures forevermore.

~ Psalm 16:11

Then shall the young women rejoice in the dance, and the young men and the old shall be merry. I will turn their mourning into joy; I will comfort them, and give them gladness for sorrow.

~ Jeremiah 31:13

"For everyone will be salted with fire."

~ Mark 9:49

*Father, please fill my day with joy and my heart with hope.*
Amen.

# 75 Live *in* Hope

We often tend to underestimate God. Or we forget that He can do the impossible; in fact, He has already done the impossible! When we experience something of the might of God, it's impossible to keep quiet about it. Then we honestly and sincerely proclaim:

- I believe because the Living God lives in me.
- I trust, because I worship an Almighty God.
- I have hope because eternal life awaits me.
- I love because He loves me endlessly.
- I witness for Him, because He intercedes for me with the Father.
- I live for Him because He died for me.

*We serve a God of the impossible.*
*Praise His holy name!*

Splendor and majesty are before Him; strength and joy are in His dwelling place. Ascribe to the LORD, all you families of nations, ascribe to the LORD glory and strength. Ascribe to the LORD the glory due His name; bring an offering and come before Him. Worship the LORD in the splendor of His holiness.

~ 1 Chronicles 16:27-29

The Sovereign LORD has given me His words of wisdom, so that I know how to comfort the weary. Morning by morning He wakens me and opens my understanding to His will.

~ Isaiah 50:4

My mouth will tell of Your righteous acts, of Your deeds of salvation all the day, for their number is past my knowledge. With the mighty deeds of the Lord God I will come; I will remind them of Your righteousness, Yours alone. O God, from my youth You have taught me, and I still proclaim Your wondrous deeds.

~ Psalm 71:15-17

*Spirit of God, let my life reflect Your glory and holiness!*
*Amen.*

# 76 A Nursery of Love

Relationships are like delicate little plants. When they're carefully planted, regularly fed and lovingly nurtured, they grow, and bloom into delightful moments in our hearts.

Such relationships are joyous flowers in the gardens of our hearts that we visit often because they refresh the soul. Unfortunately, no garden grows by itself. When we don't look after our relationships, it doesn't take long before weeds of misunderstanding, judgment, revenge and ill wishes take root and destroy them. Relationships can't survive without raindrops of love, sunshine of positive talk and a caring heart.

What do your relationships look like? Are they a wonderland of color because they are filled with seeds of care, understanding and love?

*Plant seeds of love. We serve a God of the impossible. Praise His holy Name!*

Dear friends, let us continue to love one another, for love comes from God. Anyone who loves is a child of God and knows God.

~ 1 John 4:7

Now that you have purified yourselves by obeying the truth so that you have sincere love for each other, love one another deeply, from the heart.

~ 1 Peter 1:22

Flee also youthful lusts; but pursue righteousness, faith, love, peace with those who call on the Lord out of a pure heart.

~ 2 Timothy 2:22

*Make it spring in my heart,*
*Lord, so that other people*
*will want to enter into*
*the garden of my life.*
*Amen.*

# 77 In His Time *and* His Way

**A**re you tired of praying? For years you've been asking God for some kind of change, answer, healing … and yet it feels as if He doesn't hear you. It is normal for God's children to feel discouraged when it seems like their prayers go unanswered.

The truth is that our heavenly Father lets no prayer go unanswered. Long before you even lay your requests before His throne, He already heard you … because in His love for you He understands more than just your prayers. He knows you intimately! He knows your dreams, who you are and what you need. He will answer you … but in His own time, and in His own way. Because God can see the big picture, He knows the plans He has for your future.

Time can stand still when, like Jonah, you have to wait in the stomach of a big fish. Or if you decide to fast while you wait like Esther did. But time is not important once you see the light. Or when the Light – your Savior – blesses you with His living presence.

*Sometimes God answers prayer with, "Wait a while …" because He knows what is best for you.*

Be patient, then, brothers and sisters, until the Lord's coming. See how the farmer waits for the land to yield its valuable crop, patiently waiting for the autumn and spring rains. You too, be patient and stand firm, because the Lord's coming is near.

~ James 5:7-8

The Lord is not slow in keeping His promise, as some understand slowness. Instead He is patient with you, not wanting anyone to perish, but everyone to come to repentance.

~ 2 Peter 3:9

He only is my rock and my salvation; He is my defense; I shall not be moved. In God is my salvation and my glory; the rock of my strength, and my refuge, is in God.

~ Psalm 62:6-7

*Father, thank You for answering my prayers at the perfect time and in Your perfect way.*

Amen.

# 78 A Heart of Hope

Elijah had to flee for his life after he killed King Ahab's prophets of Baal. He hid away and there, under the shade of the tree, he prayed to God and said that he had had enough of this life (see 1 Kings 19:4).

Maybe you too have felt like you just don't have the strength to carry on any more, or you wonder what the point of everything is?

If you're overcome by discouragement, and feeling like there is no hope or life has lost its spark, you are not alone. Thousands of people across the world often feel that way. Even those who walk around with a mask of confidence and smiles of pretense, experience doubt and hopelessness at times.

Remember that your heavenly Father knows every little detail about your life because He created you. He knows you better than you know yourself. Give your feelings of hopelessness to God and trust Him with it.

*With God by your side, you can travel any road. With Him darkness becomes light, a discouraged heart is filled with hope and life makes sense!*

But he himself went a day's journey into the wilderness, and came and sat down under a broom tree. And he prayed that he might die, and said, "It is enough! Now, LORD, take my life, for I am no better than my fathers!"

~ 1 Kings 19:4

The needy will not be ignored forever; the hopes of the poor will not always be crushed.

~ Psalm 9:18

Praise be to the LORD, for He has heard my cry for mercy. The LORD is my strength and my shield; my heart trusts in Him, and He helps me. My heart leaps for joy, and with my song I praise Him. The LORD is the strength of His people, a fortress of salvation for His anointed one.

~ Psalm 28:6-8

*Father, thank You for the certainty that You always listen, that You understand and that You will help me.*

Amen.

# 79 Made *in a* Special Way

It is easy to feel worthless. There will always be someone prettier, smarter, thinner, richer, more famous and more successful than you are. The irony is that even the most successful people in the world sometimes feel insecure. God doesn't want you to feel this way, because He thinks the world of you … and loves you with an eternal love!

Pray this prayer with me today:

"Lord, we are scurrying around trying to put on a great performance so that we can receive a standing ovation. But once we leave the stage, the people immediately forget about us amid their own little worlds. Tug on the puppet strings of my life, Lord, so that my life will glorify You as I serve others. I want my life's show poster to read: Tickets sold out."

*Remember the wise words of Eleanor Roosevelt*

*who said that no one can make you feel*

*inferior without your consent.*

Now thus says the Lord, He who created you, O Jacob, He who formed
you, O Israel: "Fear not, for I have
redeemed you; I have called you by
name, you are Mine."

~ Isaiah 43:1

"Can a woman forget her nursing child, and not
have compassion on the son of her womb? Surely they
may forget, yet I will not forget you. See, I have inscribed
you on the palms of My hands; your walls are continually
before Me."

~ Isaiah 49:15-16

I praise You because I am fearfully and wonderfully made; Your
works are wonderful, I know that full well. Your eyes saw my
unformed body; all the days ordained for me were written in
Your book before one of them came to be.

~ Psalm 139:14, 16

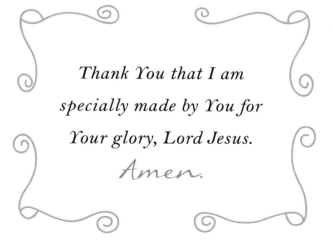

*Thank You that I am
specially made by You for
Your glory, Lord Jesus.
Amen.*

# 80 God *will* Fight for You

**C**an you remember what you were afraid of twenty, ten, or even two years ago? Did any of the things you so greatly feared ever happen?

In hindsight, you will find that the fears that stole your hope and joy weren't even worth worrying over, and that God was always with you. When you had to wade through deep waters, He carried you; when the scorching sun of life burnt down on you, He provided shade; when you were tired, He gave you a place to rest; and when you felt like running away, He lead you through the desert.

Overcome the fear of tomorrow by recalling the fears of yesterday and reminding yourself that:

- A great part of your fear is unnecessary and will never actually come true.
- Nothing can ever happen to you that you and God cannot handle together.

*God understood the fears you*
*had yesterday and helped you through.*
*He will also fight for you today and tomorrow.*

The LORD your God is going ahead of you. He will fight for you.

~ Deuteronomy 1:30

"When you pass through the waters, I will be with you; and when you pass through the rivers, they will not sweep over you. When you walk through the fire, you will not be burned; the flames will not set you ablaze."

~ Isaiah 43:2

Moses answered the people, "Do not be afraid. Stand firm and you will see the deliverance the LORD will bring you today. The Egyptians you see today you will never see again. The LORD will fight for you; you need only to be still."

~ Exodus 14:13-14

*Thank You, Lord Jesus, for understanding my fears and loving me in spite of them.*

*Amen.*

# 81 Take a Leap of Faith

Uncertainty and fear paralyze us. They dim the brightness of tomorrow. A little ray of hope could be all you need to bring about big change … to make a difference that would not have otherwise been possible.

If the Spirit of God wants you to do something or speak to someone, you can rest assured that He will help you do it. He will support you in everything you undertake. And once you step out of your comfort zone and take a leap of faith, you'll realize that it wasn't as bad as you'd thought it would be. More than that, you'll grow stronger because of it.

Listen to God's voice and take a leap of faith to the unknown. You know the One who is on your side and He will help you if you follow His will.

*Sometimes you have to do the things you're afraid of. Then you can grow and learn to trust.*

The LORD is my light and my salvation – whom shall I fear? The LORD is the stronghold of my life – of whom shall I be afraid?

~ Psalm 27:1

One night the Lord spoke to Paul in a vision and told him, "Don't be afraid! Speak out! Don't be silent! For I am with you, and no one will attack and harm you, for many people in this city belong to Me."

~ Acts 18:9-10

"So do not fear, for I am with you; do not be dismayed, for I am your God. I will strengthen you and help you; I will uphold you with My righteous right hand."

~ Isaiah 41:10

*Lord, show me what it is that You want me to do and make me obedient in it.*

*Amen.*

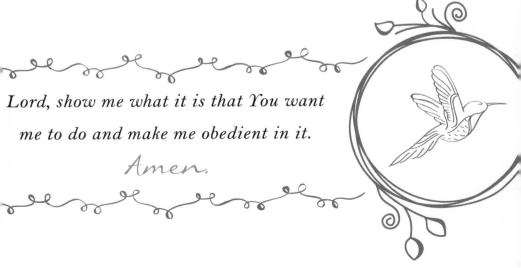

# 82 After Winter Comes *Spring*

We've all experienced winter in our hearts at some point. When it feels like our souls have been frozen and we're left bare in the bitter cold.

In times like these, it is important to remember that we serve a God who is in control of all seasons: A Father who gives joy in the summer sun, hope in the autumn, comfort during the cold winter nights and after a while … creates new life in springtime. Yes, God has a way of creating new life and joy from any situation.

Winter is not all bad, because it helps us to examine our lives closely … and sometimes to look away from ourselves so that we can see God's glory from a different perspective. It is especially during the trying winter months that He shows us His great fire of grace in our lives.

*Know that God is with you when the summer sun shines on your heart, that He too sheds tears in autumn as you grieve, and that, during those winter months, He is already busy creating new life so that you can bloom wherever He plants you.*

"God blesses you who are hungry now, for you will be satisfied. God blesses you who weep now, for in due time you will laugh."

~ Luke 6:21

The pains of death surrounded me, and the pangs of Sheol laid hold of me; I found trouble and sorrow. Then I called upon the name of the LORD: "O LORD, I implore You, deliver my soul!" Gracious is the LORD, and righteous; yes, our God is merciful. The LORD preserves the simple; I was brought low, and He saved me. Return to your rest, O my soul, for the LORD has dealt bountifully with you.

~ Psalm 116:3-7

You keep track of all my sorrows. You have collected all my tears in Your bottle. You have recorded each one in Your book. For You have rescued me from death; You have kept my feet from slipping. So now I can walk in Your presence, O God, in Your life-giving light.

~ Psalm 56:8, 13

*Creator God, I can feel the blossoms of springtime starting to bud in my heart. Thank You.*

# 83 The *Silver* Lining

During World War II, Harold Russel lost both his hands in an airplane accident. At first, he thought that his life was over. Because what can you do without hands?

He struggled with this until Charley McGonagle, who also lost his hands in World War I, came to visit him in hospital and told him what Ralph Waldo Emerson said, "For everything you have missed, you have gained something else, and for everything you gain, you lose something else." Russel was released from hospital with new hope for his future.

What are the "hands" that you've lost in your life? Is it perhaps your self-worth, career, self-dependency, financial security, energy or physical ability? Or has life stripped you of your power, energy and physical strength? Maybe your "hands" are someone whom you've loved dearly, but sadly lost.

*God fills the emptiness of loss in our lives with something new ... often with something even better. Sometimes we just need to pray that He would open our eyes to see His goodness.*

He refreshes my soul. He guides me along the right paths for His name's sake.

~ Psalm 23:3

As for me, I will always have hope; I will praise You more and more. Though You have made me see troubles, many and bitter, You will restore my life again; from the depths of the earth You will again bring me up. You will increase my honor and comfort me once more. I will praise You with the harp for Your faithfulness, my God; I will sing praise to You with the lyre, Holy One of Israel.

~ Psalm 71:14, 20-22

The LORD is good to those who wait for Him, to the soul who seeks Him.

~ Lamentations 3:25

*Lord, sometimes I am blind to the goodness all around me. Please open my eyes to see Your wonderful grace.*
*Amen.*

# 84 Choose *to* See Only the Best

The day Harold Russel lost both his hands in World War II was the start of the most successful years of his life. Shortly after his accident, he got the lead role in the film *The Best Years of Our Lives* for which he won two awards.

He also wrote an autobiography that became a best-seller. He used his new-found fame to help other disabled people. He started doing performances that changed people's lives and he discovered talents he never knew he had.

Russel later wrote that there is no formula for a happy life. But there is one simple thought: It's not what you've lost, but what you have left that matters.

Russel chose to turn his back on the pain that loss brings and instead, decided to live a happy and grateful life filled with hope … He lead a hugely successful life because of it.

*You can choose to realize your full potential today – and every day after that – with a vision and hope that the best is yet to come.*

May integrity and honesty protect me, for I put my hope in You.

~ Psalm 25:21

Praise the LORD. Blessed are those who fear the LORD, who find great delight in His commands.

~ Psalm 112:1

"The thief does not come except to steal, and to kill, and to destroy. I have come that they may have life, and that they may have it more abundantly."

~ John 10:10

One thing I do: Forgetting what is behind and straining toward what is ahead, I press on toward the goal to win the prize for which God has called me heavenward in Christ Jesus.

~ Philippians 3:13-14

*Teach me to look forward to the*
*future with great expectations, Lord.*

*Amen.*

# 85 Do *You* Still Dream?

Children have the most wonderful ability to dream. They can take a simple toy and turn it into something truly creative. You've probably also dreamed of how you wanted life to be, what you wanted to do and achieve, and what your ideal world would look like.

Quite a few of these things probably did come true and you more than likely enjoy where you are in your life right now. Yet, a lot of our expectations and dreams don't come true. What's even worse, the world has bitterly disappointed most of us and has shattered our dreams.

The beauty of it is that we can continue to dream, because there will always be new hope, opportunities, and an endless array of choices to be made. And for those who dream their dreams with God and who are willing to take it on, there will always be a second chance and another challenge.

*You are alive!* *You have a chance to seize each new day as a new opportunity: A new chance to look to the future with renewed vision and great expectations. Go out and live it to the full today!*

Jesus asked, "What is the kingdom of God like? What shall I compare it to? It is like a mustard seed, which a man took and planted in his garden. It grew and became a tree, and the birds perched in its branches."

~ Luke 13:18-19

Hope deferred makes the heart sick, but a desire fulfilled is a tree of life.

~ Proverbs 13:12

Many are the plans in a person's heart, but it is the LORD's purpose that prevails.

~ Proverbs 19:21

*Heavenly Father, I don't want to get stuck in a rut. Help me to keep dreaming with new hope and great expectation for tomorrow.*

Amen.

# 86 Peace, *Love and* Hope

It is easy to be positive when everything is going well for us. To keep it up when times are tough takes effort, intense conversations with the Spirit of God and strong willpower. When you find yourself spiraling into an abyss of negative thoughts, stop and do the following:

- *Accept* that you may have lost a few things and choose to focus on what you have left.
- *Stop blaming yourself.* You will sometimes make mistakes, learn from them and decide to do it differently next time. Give yourself credit for what you're doing right and build on that.
- *Don't blame others.* Blame will get you nowhere. See the past as over and decide what you can do to make the best of any given situation.
- *Forgive, forgive and forgive some more.* An unforgiving spirit makes you a prisoner of your own thoughts. It's never worth it.

*Pray that God's Spirit will give you peace, love and hope in your heart.*

Make every effort to live in peace with everyone and to be holy; without holiness no one will see the Lord.

~ Hebrews 12:14

The mind governed by the flesh is death, but the mind governed by the Spirit is life and peace.

~ Romans 8:6

Grace to you and peace from God our Father and the Lord Jesus Christ.

~ 1 Corinthians 1:3

"Peace I leave with you, My peace I give to you; not as the world gives do I give to you. Let not your heart be troubled, neither let it be afraid."

~ John 14:27

*God of peace, help me to focus on Your love in any and every situation I have to face.*

*Amen.*

# 87 You Are His *Child*!

"I'm going through a really difficult time and it feels like God is far away from me. Has He forgotten about me?" the desperate message showed up on my phone. My friend was going through a difficult time. You might have gone through a dry spell where you were left wondering whether God truly loved you enough to want to be with you.

In such times it is helpful to read the book of Habakkuk and see how frustrated and tired he was of begging God. He so badly wanted God to save his people from the Babylonians. It looked as if the enemy would get away with murder while God turned a blind eye. But then God answered him: "This vision is for a future time. It describes the end, and it will be fulfilled. If it seems slow in coming, wait patiently, for it will surely take place. It will not be delayed" (Hab. 2:3).

Although God does not immediately take their suffering away, Habakkuk knew that God would never forsake His children during difficult times, or allow the enemy to overpower them.

*Remember today that you are His child!*
*That is why He will keep you safe, even when*
*you're traveling through rough terrain.*

To all who did receive Him, who believed in His name, He gave the right to become children of God.

~ John 1:12

I am counting on the LORD; yes, I am counting on Him. I have put my hope in His word. I long for the Lord more than sentries long for the dawn, yes, more than sentries long for the dawn.

~ Psalm 130:5-6

Therefore I will look to the LORD; I will wait for the God of my salvation; my God will hear me.

~ Micah 7:7

He makes my feet like the feet of a deer; He causes me to stand on the heights. He trains my hands for battle; my arms can bend a bow of bronze.

~ Psalm 18:33-34

*Faithful Father,*
*make my feet like the*
*feet of a deer standing*
*firm on the heights.*
*Amen.*

# 88 "Even though ..."

Each and every one of us has a fig tree in our lives. There are times when things are going well and the branches of our hearts are hanging heavy with fruit. Then there are times when it feels like we're living futile and fruitless lives: when nothing seems to work out.

Then we start to doubt ourselves, others and life, and we lose all hope. At other times, we experience dry seasons. Of course there are days when the storms of life threaten to uproot us, and leave us wondering where our help will come from.

On those days it is good to read about Habakkuk's struggles and how he learned to trust God. He decided that, even though his future looked bleak and all hope was lost, he would keep hoping and believing. He chose to believe despite everything, and to keep praising God even during the dry seasons of his life.

*Pray that you will always be able to rejoice in the fact that you are saved and that, in spite of everything, God will help you.*

Even though the fig trees have no blossoms, and there are no grapes on the vines; even though the olive crop fails, and the fields lie empty and barren; even though the flocks die in the fields, and the cattle barns are empty, yet I will rejoice in the LORD! I will be joyful in the God of my salvation!

~ Habakkuk 3:17-18

Sing the praises of the LORD, enthroned in Zion; proclaim among the nations what He has done.

~ Psalm 9:11

Let me hear in the morning of Your steadfast love, for in You I trust. Make me know the way I should go, for to You I lift up my soul.

~ Psalm 143:8

Though He slay me, yet will I trust Him.

~ Job 13:15

*Lord, with Habakkuk*
*I declare today that You*
*are my strength even though*
*the fig tree has no blossoms.*
*Amen.*

# 89 The *Doorway* to Eternity

To live without God is to live an empty life. To die without God is frightening. It is said that the death of Stalin – the man responsible for the death of 80 million Russians (mostly Christians) – was a horrible sight to see.

His daughter said that it was a nightmare to watch her father die. Lenin on the other hand, died after a night of spiritual hopelessness where he frantically pleaded for the forgiveness of his sins. There are many stories of atheists who became terribly frightened on their death beds … some even called out to God for His mercy and forgiveness.

Born-again children of God die differently. They enter eternal life with peace because they know that death is nothing to fear. They are fully aware that death is only the doorway to an eternity with their heavenly Father.

We cannot choose where, when or how we will die, but as long as we live, we have time to choose how we will feel when we die.

*To enter into eternal life*
*with God brings true peace and serenity.*

When the perishable puts on the imperishable, and the mortal puts on immortality, then shall come to pass the saying that is written: "Death is swallowed up in victory."

~ 1 Corinthians 15:54

The path of the righteous is like the morning sun, shining ever brighter till the full light of day. But the way of the wicked is like deep darkness; they do not know what makes them stumble.

~ Proverbs 4:18-19

"Finally, the poor man died and was carried by the angels to sit beside Abraham at the heavenly banquet. The rich man also died and was buried, and he went to the place of the dead. There, in torment, he saw Abraham in the far distance with Lazarus at his side."

~ Luke 16:22-23

*Father, I want to spend every moment of this life and the afterlife with You. Help me to persevere.*

*Amen.*

# 90 Exchange Fear *for* Love

If we are honest with ourselves, we will admit that people scare us. That is why so many of us find it absolutely terrifying to get up and speak in front of others. We find it just as difficult to confront someone or talk about an uncomfortable situation. But when we speak sincerely from the heart, the Spirit of God makes that fear disappear.

When you find yourself in a difficult situation outside of your comfort zone, don't allow it to steal your joy or your hope. Remember the universal language of love!

Remember Paul's words: "Love is patient, love is kind. It does not envy, it does not boast, it is not proud. It does not dishonor others, it is not self-seeking, it is not easily angered, it keeps no record of wrongs. Love does not delight in evil but rejoices with the truth" (1 Cor. 13:4-6).

*Exchange your fear of people for love.*
*You will discover that your words will flow*
*naturally and that the end result is positive.*

Love never gives up, never loses faith, is always hopeful, and endures through every circumstance.

~ 1 Corinthians 13:7

God is not unjust; He will not forget your work and the love you have shown Him as you have helped His people and continue to help them.

~ Hebrews 6:10

There is no fear in love; but perfect love casts out fear, because fear involves torment. But he who fears has not been made perfect in love.

~ 1 John 4:18

*Holy Spirit, help me to speak and act from a heart filled with Your love.*

*Amen.*

# 91 Life Is *not* Always Fair

It doesn't matter how hard we try to lead good and honorable lives, sometimes life just isn't fair. Then you wonder: Does it even help to be faithful? What use is it to live righteously and lovingly when life is so unfair?

Ask yourself: Were the people who stoned Stephen to death righteous? Did Paul, after all the good he had done, deserve to be thrown in prison? Did Jesus deserve to be crucified?

The answers to these questions help us realize that life doesn't always give us what we deserve. And we are not in control of what happens to us. But the Word does tell us is that the pain and heartache of the world cannot take away God's goodness, faithfulness and promises to us.

*God is forever faithful. He is faithful in the way He carries us through difficult times. He is faithful in His love and in His promise that He will one day come again to judge each person in righteousness.*

While we live in these earthly bodies, we groan and sigh, but it's not that we want to die and get rid of these bodies that clothe us. Rather, we want to put on our new bodies so that these dying bodies will be swallowed up by life.

~ 2 Corinthians 5:4

Good and upright is the LORD; therefore He instructs sinners in His ways. He guides the humble in what is right and teaches them His way. All the ways of the LORD are loving and faithful toward those who keep the demands of His covenant.

~ Psalm 25:8-10

In You, O LORD, I put my trust; let me never be put to shame. Deliver me in Your righteousness, and cause me to escape; incline Your ear to me, and save me. Be my strong refuge, to which I may resort continually; You have given the commandment to save me, for You are my rock and my fortress.

~ Psalm 71:1-3

*Father of heaven and earth, I put my hope and trust in You today.*

*Amen.*

# 92 Believe the Best About People

The Great Architect of Love did not exactly tell us how we should live in love, but He did give us clear guidelines for love. God's love says:

- *Believe the best about others.* Jesus believed in an outcast, a tax collector, and by doing so turned him into a hero. What is keeping you from seeing the good and beautiful in others?
- *Hope for the best in others.* If God had wanted to, He could have given up on us a long time ago. But He didn't. Do you give people hope in the way that you love them?
- *Accept others.* God might not always like us, but He will never stop loving us. How often do you love others despite their flaws?

*When you see someone through God's eyes, you'll receive the understanding, patience and wisdom to truly love them.*

Love bears all things, believes all things, hopes all things, endures all things.

~ 1 Corinthians 13:7

No one has ever seen God; but if we love one another, God lives in us and His love is made complete in us.

~ 1 John 4:12

Do everything in love.

~ 1 Corinthians 16:14

Also for this very reason, giving all diligence, add to your faith virtue, to virtue knowledge, to knowledge self-control, to self-control perseverance, to perseverance godliness, to godliness brotherly kindness, and to brotherly kindness love.

~ 2 Peter 1:5-7

*Father, teach me to love in a way*
*that believes in others, hopes in them*
*and accepts them as You do.*
*Amen.*

# 93 Father *of the* Abandoned

We've all experienced it before. That feeling of abandonment. Maybe at one stage you were abandoned and it has left a big scar on your heart. Or maybe it was just something someone said or did that made you feel pushed to the side.

Like Hagar, the woman who expected Abraham's first child, Ishmael, after his wife Sarah insisted on it and who later was chased away by the same Sarah.

Hagar and her small child found themselves kicked out of their home. They ended up in the desert where they nearly died of thirst and hunger. A sad tale of an abandoned woman stripped of all hope … until God stepped in.

God sees this abandoned woman and sends His angel to give her hope and to convince her that He will not let her or her son down: "Arise, lift up the lad and hold him with your hand, for I will make him a great nation" (Gen. 21:18).

*Find hope and comfort in the fact that our God is the Father of abandoned and outcast people.*

"But to you who fear My name the Sun of Righteousness shall arise with healing in His wings; and you shall go out and grow fat like stall-fed calves."

~ Malachi 4:2

The LORD watches over the foreigner and sustains the fatherless and the widow, but He frustrates the ways of the wicked.

~ Psalm 146:9

The righteous person faces many troubles, but the LORD comes to the rescue each time.

~ Psalm 34:19

"Behold! My Servant whom I uphold, My Elect One in whom My soul delights! I have put My Spirit upon Him; He will bring forth justice to the Gentiles. A bruised reed He will not break, and smoking flax He will not quench; He will bring forth justice for truth."

~ Isaiah 42:1, 3

*Immanuel, God with us,*
*thank You that I can find comfort*
*and healing in Your sweet embrace.*
*Amen.*

# 94 It's *not* About Us

**B**elievers can easily fall into the trap of expectations. We can easily think that because we believe in God, faithfully worship Him and do things for Him, He owes us something. But we are quick to become angry when we feel that God is not living up to our expectations. These are the moments when our faith revolves around us alone.

The truth about faith is in fact that it is all about the holy, omniscient God. Without God there is nothing: No expectation or future. That is why Eugenia Price said that faith should follow this order:

- God, who is always there, comes first.
- Second is our hope and trust in God. Even when He feels far away, He is still with you.
- Only then … comes our feelings. Because feelings can be deceiving.

*If you sometimes feel like God can't be trusted, read Psalm 34 and remember that God, despite our changing emotions, remains the same. That is why He will remain unshakable and faithful for eternity.*

Taste and see that the L<small>ORD</small> is good; blessed is the one who takes refuge in Him. The lions may grow weak and hungry, but those who seek the L<small>ORD</small> lack no good thing.

~ Psalm 34:8, 10

These have come so that the proven genuineness of your faith – of greater worth than gold, which perishes even though refined by fire – may result in praise, glory and honor when Jesus Christ is revealed.

~ 1 Peter 1:7

We have come to share in Christ, if indeed we hold our original conviction firmly to the very end.

~ Hebrews 3:14

*Lord, help me to think about You as the true and eternal Father who is always faithful. Especially when I'm in doubt.*

*Amen.*

# 95 Lily of the Valley

It is a full-time exercise to shake off negativity and to focus on the positive. Especially if it's all about you. Because the negative powers of Satan are so active in our lives, we can only change our way of thinking with the help of the Holy Spirit.

Pray every day for:

- Protection against evil. Know that as a child of God you can come under attack, but know that the Holy Spirit will protect you.
- The forgiveness of your sins. And remember that when you repent in humble sincerity, God forgives. Don't allow anyone to tell you otherwise.
- The fulfilment of the truth. There is only one truth – God's truth. Allow His Spirit to fill you with His positive and loving messages every day.
- Your acceptance of the truth. Ask your Shepherd to help you go out and live as the unique, special person that you are.

*The next time you feel overwhelmed by feelings of worthlessness, guilt or negativity, keep hoping and remember God's wonderful promises of abundance.*

His branches shall spread; His beauty shall be like an olive tree, and his fragrance like Lebanon. Those who dwell under His shadow shall return; they shall be revived like grain, and grow like a vine. Their scent shall be like the wine of Lebanon.

~ Hosea 14:6-7

I remain confident of this: I will see the goodness of the LORD in the land of the living. Wait for the LORD; be strong and take heart and wait for the LORD.

~ Psalm 27:13-14

I will sing to the LORD because He is good to me.

~ Psalm 13:6

*Father, help me to bloom*

*in the love You have for me.*

*Amen.*

# 96 There Is *Only* One Answer

Are you stuck in a tight grip of anxiety and panic? Does it feel like fear shrinks your heart and you can't breathe? During such times life seems out of control and we feel uncertain about the future. We keep asking "What if ..." It is highly likely that we start witnessing how everything turns out wrong.

When I read Psalm 27, I sense something of this in David. It is as if he felt overwhelmed by his situation and begged God for help. Then, after a long time struggling, when he finally laid his heart bare before God, he came to this insight: "Though a mighty army surrounds me, my heart will not be afraid. Even if I am attacked, I will remain confident" (Ps. 27:3). In verse 14, he ends with an encouraging message: "Wait patiently for the LORD. Be brave and courageous. Yes, wait patiently for the LORD." Fear is a universal feeling. Trust in God is a privilege that we have as His children. You are His dearly beloved child.

*In times of fear, like David, remember:*
*Even though my mother and father leave me,*
*God the Father will hold me close.*

God has said, "Never will I leave you; never will I forsake you."

~ Hebrews 13:5

I am convinced that nothing can ever separate us from God's love. Neither death nor life, neither angels nor demons, neither our fears for today nor our worries about tomorrow – not even the powers of hell can separate us from God's love.

~ Romans 8:38

The LORD has taken away your punishment, He has turned back your enemy. The LORD, the King of Israel, is with you; never again will you fear any harm.

~ Zephaniah 3:15

*Lord, I put my entire life in Your hands with the hope and certainty that You will always be faithful.*

*Amen.*

# 97 He *Will Quiet* Your Heart

**M**ore than 95% of the things you worry about never happen. That is why it is so unnecessary to waste valuable time worrying – it just steals your hope and joy. Yet we remain doubtful, we wonder and often expect the worst to happen.

When stress and worry overwhelm you, there is one steadfast solution: intense prayer and meditation on God's Word. There at His feet, you'll find a different perspective and the flame of hope will burn stronger than ever. When you allow the Spirit to fill you and His Word to strengthen you, you will experience how God in a supernatural way brings you rest. He will calm your heart and assure you that He will always be in control of your life.

You'll realize that nothing on earth that might happen to you, can make any difference to your eternal status in heaven. Put into perspective, you'll realize that even five years from now it wouldn't have had that much of an impact in your life.

*"What if" will probably never ever happen. And if it does, the Father will give you the strength, wisdom and grace you need to deal with it.*

So we fix our eyes not on what is seen, but on what is unseen, since what is seen is temporary, but what is unseen is eternal.

~ 2 Corinthians 4:18

Worry weighs a person down; an encouraging word cheers a person up.

~ Proverbs 12:25

Cast all your anxiety on Him because He cares for you.

~ 1 Peter 5:7

*Father, thank You for helping*
*me to overcome my human fears.*

*Amen.*

# 98 Focus *on* His Light

Just think how bored we would have been with life if everything followed the same monotonous pattern every day. But, you'll probably agree that you wouldn't mind a few ordinary days in your life. Because problems, frustrations and drama have a way of rolling in around us like thunder clouds.

That the world will sometimes be confusing, chaotic and frustrating is a fact. That we will sometimes go through difficult times is true. But it isn't always bad for us. Difficult times are often the best time for growth. It is during such times that we start to look at the world differently again.

When we pray, we should therefore not ask God for an easy life. We should rather pray that He would, under any circumstances, give us the wisdom we need, that He will carry us through the difficulties and frustration, and that He will grant us a lot more patience.

*May you experience the Father's guiding light and hope in the dark of night.*

Then the LORD will create over the whole site of Mount Zion and over her assemblies a cloud by day, and smoke and the shining of a flaming fire by night; for over all the glory there will be a canopy. There will be a booth for shade by day from the heat, and for a refuge and a shelter from the storm and rain.

~ Isaiah 4:5-6

The LORD will guide you always; He will satisfy your needs in a sun-scorched land and will strengthen your frame. You will be like a well-watered garden, like a spring whose waters never fail.

~ Isaiah 58:11

Show me the right path, O LORD; point out the road for me to follow. Lead me by Your truth and teach me, for You are the God who saves me. All day long I put my hope in You.

~ Psalm 25:4-5

*Lord of Light,*
*help me to focus on*
*You alone no matter*
*the circumstances.*
*Amen.*

# 99 Be a "Yes" person

We get a lot of "No's" from a young age. When we feel adventurous or take chances, Mother's "No!" stops us in our tracks. When we think that we're the smartest, prettiest girl in the world, other people's feedback might suggest the opposite.

During the teenage years, few of us get to look in the mirror and see the "ideal" image the magazines advertise. And so we learn to naturally say "No" every time God wants to encourage us to be more.

If you feel like this, the time has come for you to become deaf to the world and to brush off all the no's and you-can't-do-it's. Yes, maybe now is the time to believe like a little girl that you are more than good enough. You are great!

*Pray that the Spirit will wipe away all the negative voices in your head and that He will place a new you – the true you – in its place.*

This I recall to my mind, therefore I have hope. Through the LORD's mercies we are not consumed, because His compassions fail not. They are new every morning.

~ Lamentations 3:21-23

"On the day when I act," says the LORD Almighty, "they will be My treasured possession. I will spare them, just as a father has compassion and spares his son who serves him."

~ Malachi 3:17

You are a chosen generation, a royal priest-hood, a holy nation, His own special people, that you may proclaim the praises of Him who called you out of darkness into His marvelous light."

~ 1 Peter 2:9

*Father, take away all the*
*uncertainties of the past, and*
*help me to live out the true*
*version of me with a heart*
*filled with hope.*
*Amen.*

# 100 Choose to Trust Him

There are so many things that upset us. We live in a world where things go wrong, accidents and disasters happen, and the future is a mystery. The only thing we can be sure of is change.

There is one place that you and I can feel safe amid the storm; where we can find rest in spite of the unsteady world and where we can find certainty in uncertain times. It is at the feet of our Master – the God who, in spite of everything, always stays the same and always remains in control. Choose today not to:

- get upset when you read the newspaper headlines
- feel uncertain and scared about your future
- panic when things don't go according to plan
- allow unrest to steal your joy.

Choose to remember that once you live in accordance with God's will, He remains in control of your life.

*Because God guides you and holds you in the palm of His hand, He will make everything work out for your good.*

The word of the Lord is proven; He is a shield to all who trust in Him.

~ Psalm 18:30

Trust in Him at all times, you people; pour out your hearts to Him, for God is our refuge. Surely the lowborn are but a breath, the highborn are but a lie. If weighed on a balance, they are nothing; together they are only a breath.

~ Psalm 62:8-9

Don't worry about anything; instead, pray about everything. Tell God what you need, and thank Him for all he has done. Then you will experience God's peace, which exceeds anything we can understand. His peace will guard your hearts and minds as you live in Christ Jesus.

~ Philippians 4:6-7

*Father God, I choose today to trust in You with all my heart.*

*Amen.*

# 101 From the Ash Heap *to* Heavenly *Hope*

There is no shame in sitting on the rubbish heap every now and again. Some of God's biggest heroes often swung by there. To feel hopeless, depressed and lost is human emotions we all experience sooner or later.

Fortunately, with the help of the Holy Spirit, most of us are able to find our way out of the pit of depression. But sometimes things happen that have a longer lasting and bigger effect on us. At times like these we need more help, like the faithful ear of a friend, a psychologist or maybe even medical assistance.

When you realize that your days of depression have become a pattern over which you have no control, you know that the time has come to seek help from outside. God uses medical and psychological help to help us see the light again.

*God wants all of us to be positive and happy people with a spring in our step and hope in our hearts. Do something about it if you battle with darkness constantly.*

I cried out, "I am slipping!" but Your unfailing love, O LORD, supported me. When doubts filled my mind, Your comfort gave me renewed hope and cheer.

~ Psalm 94:18-19

O my God, my soul is cast down within me; therefore I will remember You from the land of the Jordan, and from the heights of Hermon, from the Hill Mizar. Deep calls unto deep at the noise of Your waterfalls; all Your waves and billows have gone over me.

~ Psalm 42:6-7

Please listen, God, and answer my prayer! I feel hopeless, and I cry out to You from a faraway land. Lead me to the mighty rock high above me. You are a strong tower, where I am safe.

~ Psalm 61:1-3

*Lord Jesus, show me where*
*to go for help and hope*
*when I can't lift myself*
*from the pit of despair.*
*Amen.*

# Scripture Verses *for Specific* Needs

God created your inmost being. He understands all your needs. Whatever it is that you seek or long for, the Bible offers hope and help. Use this thematic Scripture guide when you need guidance and comfort. God will provide in your daily needs in a wonderful way!

## Adoration
Romans 11:34
Isaiah 49:23
Psalm 126:1-3

## Blessing
Psalm 41:2
Matthew 5:8
Psalm 8:5-6

## Character
Ephesians 4:15
Titus 2:3-5
Proverbs 2:6-7

## Comfort
Psalm 16:8-9
Zephaniah 3:17
Daniel 9:23

## Compassion
Matthew 7:12
Lamentations 3:21-23
Revelation 21:4
Psalm 103:8-11

## Contentment
Proverbs 19:23
Psalm 147:11
Psalm 23:4

## Courage
Psalm 34:5, 9
Ephesians 1:18
Hebrews 10:35-36

## Deliverance
Exodus 14:13
Isaiah 53:4
Psalm 91:4

## Encouragement
Ephesians 1:19
1 Thessalonians 5:11
Romans 12:15

## Eternal Life
Philippians 1:6
Philippians 1:9-10
Romans 1:20

## Faith
2 Corinthians 5:7
2 Peter 1:17
Galatians 5:25

## Faithfulness
1 Corinthians 1:9
Hebrews 13:5
Matthew 6:30

## Favor

Matthew 5:3
Psalm 31:15-16
Romans 8:11

## Fear

Psalm 34:9
2 Timothy 1:7
Genesis 15:1

## Friendship

Proverbs 18:24
Proverbs 17:17
Proverbs 27:9

## Gods Love

Proverbs 3:12
1 John 4:10
Exodus 20:6

## Grace

Ephesians 4:7
2 Corinthians 12:9
1 Peter 4:10
John 1:16

## Guidance

Psalm 37:23-24
Isaiah 30:21
Psalm 23:1-2

## Help

Psalm 146:5
Matthew 8:26
Romans 8:26

## Holy Spirit

John 14:15-17
1 Corinthians 14:12
Ephesians 1:14

## Hope

Romans 5:5
1 Thessalonians 1:3
Hebrews 6:19-20

## Humility

1 Peter 5:6-7
Proverbs 2:6-7
Psalm 31:23

## Inheritance

Ephesians 1:14
Ephesians 1:18
Isaiah 43:1

## Joy

Psalm 146:1-2
Ecclesiastes 11:9
Psalm 128:P1-2

## Love

1 John 4:12
John 15:9
Jeremiah 31:3

## Mercy

Matthew 5:7
Ephesians 2:4-5
Jude 20-21

## Obedience

Matthew 28:20
Psalm 119:165-166
Acts 7:60

## Patience

Proverbs 16:32
James 5:7-8
2 Peter 3:9

## Peace

1 Peter 1:2
Romans 5:1

## Perseverance

Galatians 6:9
Galatians 5:1
James 1:12

## Praise

Isaiah 12:5
Psalm 63:2, 4-5
Psalm 139:13-14

## Promises

Luke 24:49
Genesis 9:13-15
Psalm 146:6

## Prosperity

Luke 19:16-17
Matthew 6:8
Psalm 52:8

## Protection

Deuteronomy 5:5
Exodus 14:14
Psalm 86:2

## Provision

Philippians 4:19
Psalm 36:8
Philippians 4:19

## Purpose

Ephesians 2:9-10
Jeremiah 29:11

## Refuge

Psalm 16:8
Psalm 36:6-7

## Rest

Matthew 11:28-29
Mark 6:31
Psalm 37:7

## Restoration

Isaiah 57:15
Luke 17:5
Isaiah 58:11

## Righteous Living

Proverbs 4:23-24
Psalm 51:12
2 Timothy 2:22

## Salvation

Isaiah 12:2
Psalm 68:20-21
Galatians 5:1

## Servitude

1 Peter 4:10
2 Chronicles 15:7
Hebrews 14:14

## Strength

Isaiah 40:31
1 Chronicles 16:10-12, 14
Ephesians 6:10

## Suffering

1 Peter 1:6
1 Timothy 4:10
Psalm 138:7

## Success

Psalm 92:13-16
Mark 11:22-23
1 Corinthians 15:37-38

## Thankfulness

Jeremiah 33:11
Psalm 139:14, 16
Psalm 71:14, 20-22

## Trials

Psalm 42:11
Romans 5:3-4
Hebrews 10:38

## Trust

Proverbs 3:5-6
Psalm 112:6-7
Matthew 19:26

## Victory

Romans 8:37
1 Corinthians 15:57
2 Timothy 4:7-8

## Wisdom

Ecclesiastes 8:5-6
Proverbs 23:17-19
Ephesians 5:15-16

## Work

Proverbs 31:17-18, 25
Joel 2:28
Psalm 37:4

# Notes

# Notes

# Notes